Yosemite Reverie

Thomas A. Richman

Yosemite Reverie

copyright © 2020 by Thomas A. Richman

Printed in the United States of America

All Rights Reserved

Published by Thomas A. Richman

PO Box 511270

Penngrove, California 94951

ISBN 978-0-578-67412-4 (paperback)

This book has been composed in Adobe Caslon Pro.

*To the One
who writes these words
and reads these words
and longs to know itself.*

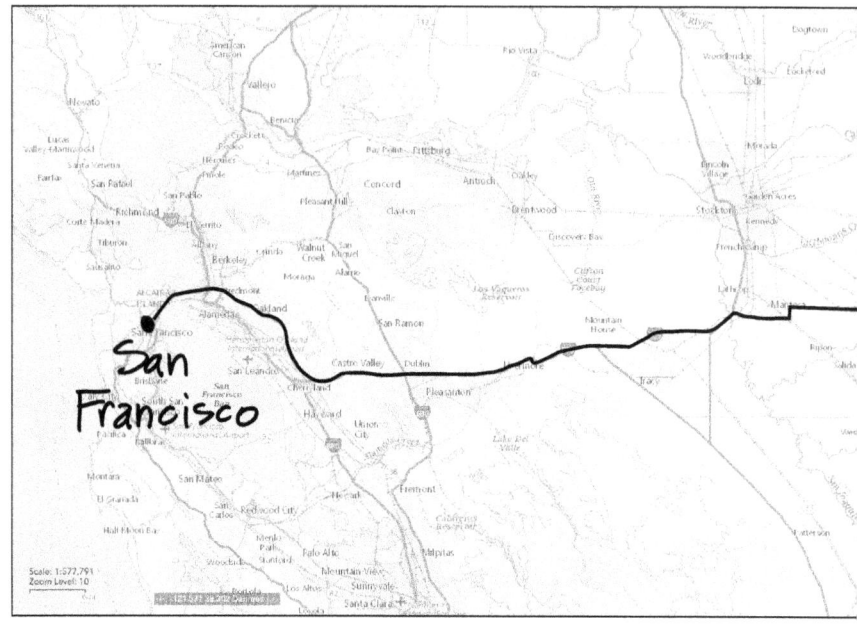

San Fransicso to Yosemite National Park, Tuolumne Meadows Visitor Center
217 miles [350 km], about five hours

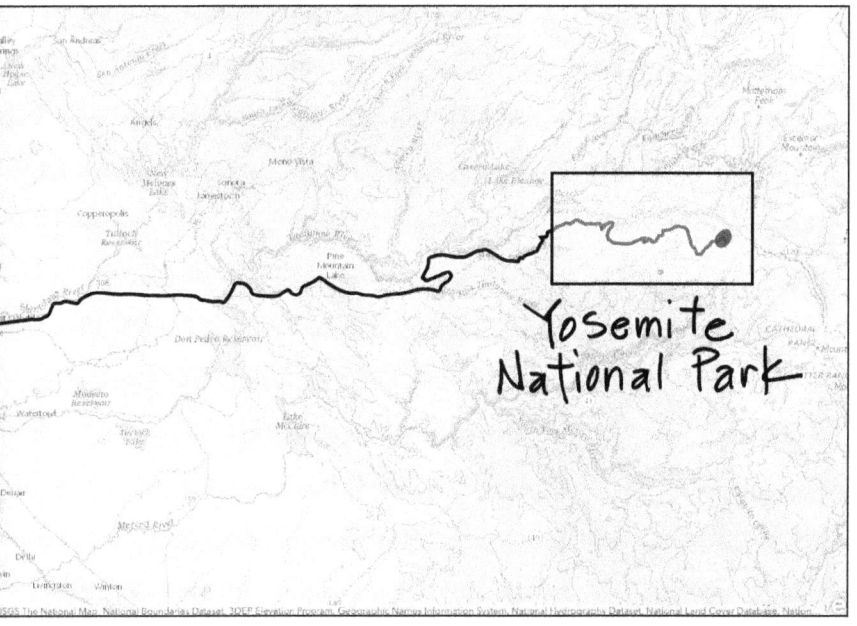

YOSEMITE NATIONAL PARK

... a shrine to human foresight, the strength of granite, the power of glaciers, the persistence of life, and the tranquility of the High Sierra.

First protected in 1864, Yosemite National Park is best known for its waterfalls, but within its nearly 1,200 square miles, you can find deep valleys, grand meadows, ancient giant sequoias, a vast wilderness area, and much more. . . .

— United States National Park Service

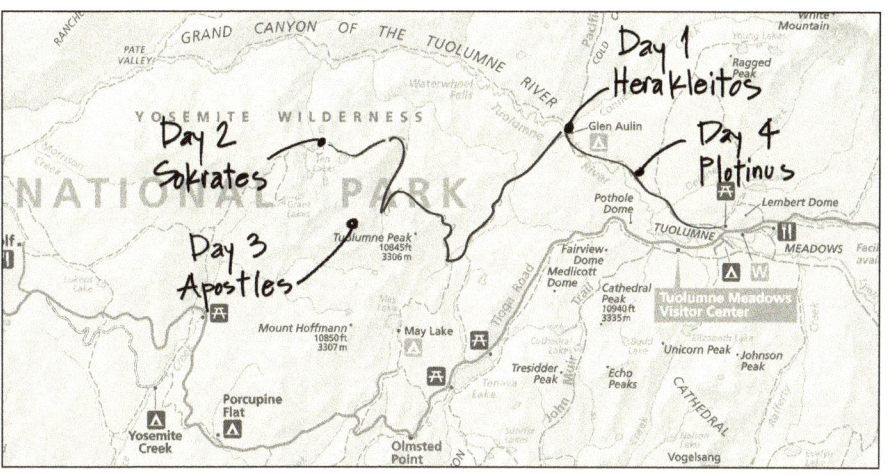

I only went out for a walk, and finally concluded to stay out
till sundown, for going out, I found, was really going in.
— *The Unpublished Journals of John Muir* c. 1893

Contents

I. Ascent 1
II. Glen Aulin 25
III. Ten Lakes 40
IV. Bhog Joonni 92
V. Smith Peak 105
VI. Return 141

Endnotes. 184

Introduction

Author's Note

A reverie is a state of being lost in one's thoughts, a daydream, a vision — even a hallucination. The work before us may be all that, but it is also something more: an invitation, an exploration and a revelation.

This little book invites us to enter a new world, a higher perspective, a broader horizon. This new world offers an escape from the relentless, restless cacophony of modern life and an entrance into the relaxed, quiet, profound rhythms of nature. To enter this world is to disconnect from the reactive, instant superficial communication of our age, and instead commune with the oldest, most meaningful messages drawn from the deepest well of human consciousness.

Set in the Sierra Nevada, this book explores not only a particular place — what naturalist John Muir called "The Range of Light" — with its granite rocks, howling winds, soaring birds and crashing waterfalls — but also one person's quest for light.

Yosemite Reverie

By walking with him as he explores the fundamental questions — who am I? why am I here? where will I go? — we are drawn into our own exploration.

The narrator makes no assertions, draws no conclusions. Like many who set out to find certainty, he comes to realize that, in the words of the poet Rilke, joy lies not in finding the answers, but in living the questions.

This book is above all a revelation — a revelation that the spiritual awareness we seek is not far away, not locked in some distant fortress which must be breached, not something to be achieved, but something to which we open, something that is happening to us.

It's as natural as the flowering of a delicate blossom, or the emergence of a towering mountain from the level plain. It takes time, it may be barely perceptible within our frame of reference, but if we are still, if we filter out the noise, and focus on the signal, we become aware — like the teller of this story — of the great pulse of life, ever-flowing, always present, evergreen.

This book arises out of my own experience of more than forty years of relationship with a living master, daily meditation practice, and study of spiritual literature, but it's not a memoir. It's not a treatise. It's a story.

Introduction

Like Alice's *Looking Glass,* Harry Potter's *Platform Nine and Three Quarters,* or the Scottish standing stones in the Starz TV series "Outlander," the wilderness of the high Sierra serves as a portal to another world. Yes, there's philosophy and history and wisdom from ancient teachers, but there are bears and storms and adventures, too.

Though the setting and context of the narrator's encounters may be imaginary, *every word of philosophy or spirituality spoken by the ancients is a direct quote from primary source material,* retranslated to be more accessible to modern readers. The *Endnotes* and *Bibliography* make it easy for those interested in deeper study to consult the original texts.

The primary insight of the *Reverie* is that there's no Eastern or Western philosophy, no ancient or modern teaching — just one radiant truth, delivered with consistency by teachers of all times, present to each one of us now.

Thomas A. Richman
Shanti Bagh West
Penngrove, California

I. Ascent

Yosemite Reverie

1

Another long, grueling day.

Conference calls. Long, boring meetings. Delays and cost overruns. Would we ever get ahead of the bills? Lunch at my desk, as usual, trying to keep up with email. Barely a few minutes of quiet to actually think.

Time to go home.

I packed up my laptop, stuffed a few files into my satchel to look at in the evening and said goodnight to my assistant.

"See you tomorrow," he said.

"Tomorrow, yes, see you. G'night."

I rode the elevator down four floors and stepped out on the sidewalk. Another glorious San Francisco evening. What's the point of living in everybody's favorite city if I'm trapped in cubeland all day? I thought, at least I have the ten minute walk from the office to the condo. I waited at the corner.

I was thinking about tomorrow's meetings when the light turned green and I stepped off. Mid-step a voice inside told me: *look left*.

Ascent

A silver BMW bore down on me, the driver with one hand on the wheel and the other holding a phone, roaring through the red. I drew back and felt a whack against my left wrist — a shot of pain up my arm — a metal and glass blur — and the Beemer speed away, the passenger side mirror folded back on its hinge.

"Man, that was close," a bike messenger leaning on the light pole said, taking out his earbuds, "you alright?"

"Yes, yes, I'm OK," I said, voice shaking, rubbing my wrist where it hit the mirror.

"Happens all the time," said a girl with spiky hair and a rose tattoo twining around her neck, holding out an arm to steady me, "they're, like, all in a rush for the Bay Bridge. You good?"

"Yes," I said as I tried to catch my breath, "thank you."

"OK, man, you take care," she said.

Our moment of human connection ended as abruptly as it began. They rushed across the street and disappeared. I waited through another cycle, shook my arm to take the sting off, collected myself, and then, at the next green, cautiously stepped out — looking carefully in each direction, twice — and gingerly traversed the crosswalk. Then another, and another, and another, until I arrived home.

YOSEMITE REVERIE

2

At the lobby I collected the mail — nothing interesting. I tossed most of it in the recycle bin by the elevator door. When it opened I pushed "10" and was carried up.

I threw my bag on the kitchen chair, dropped the remaining mail in the inbox, and filled the kettle. With the whistle I made a cup of chamomile to calm my nerves and moved to the window behind the sofa, cradling the warm mug. We had a Bay view when we bought the place, but didn't realize at the time the parking lot across the street would become another high rise apartment building. Now I faced a steel and glass slab and a roaring street below.

That was close. What if I had stepped off? What if I had died today?

I felt the sting in my wrist, where the car mirror hit, and noticed the lens of my watch was cracked and the movement had stopped — *6:17*. I was literally out of time.

They say when you die, your whole life passes before you. I wasn't sure about that, but there, looking out the window, drinking warm tea, I looked back on mine.

Ascent

I remembered being a lonely only child growing up in a three-bedroom middle-class suburban house on the big flat prairie in the middle of North America. When winter is so cold that snot freezes on your face, you don't have the luxury of magical thinking. There's no place for fantasy. You have to be practical, on purpose. Dream and die.

One night when I was about ten, drifting off to sleep in my cozy bedroom, I began to think about dying and being dead. When you're dead, you're dead forever, I thought. How long is that?

Is it a million years? A billion? A billion billion? A gazillion? The ten year old brain tried to stretch out to the longest time it could imagine. But still it didn't seem long enough. No, it's longer than that. It's forever, and forever, *and forever*....

I repeated "...and forever, and forever" to myself. I kept it up for a long time. I tried to repeat "and forever" with all of my attention, focusing really hard. Something prompted me to keep repeating, as if by repeating these words continuously, I would somehow be able to grasp the enormity of eternity.

Then, with "forever and forever and forever and forever and forever" rolling, I suddenly broke through into a blue-black sky full of stars. There was nothing but space and stars and me — not the ten-year old physical me lying in the bed, but the conscious entity that I called myself — floating freely in a limitless void filled with countless points of light.

Yosemite Reverie

I was one with the universe. I was in a timeless, limitless, spaceless space. I had expanded into an infinite sky and contracted deep into myself at the same time. Somehow I was dead to myself — "I" did not exist — yet I was fully conscious and aware of a greater universe than I had ever imagined.

I don't know how long this cosmic oneness lasted. But as soon as I had a thought — *what is happening to me?* — it was gone.

I leapt out of bed in terror, ran downstairs to where my parents were watching the blaring TV.

"Mommy, daddy, I don't wanna die!" I screamed.

"Don't worry, honey," my mother said. She looked away from the screen for a moment, and refocused her eyes on mine. In that moment she confronted one of the hardest choices a parent can face — to be honest, or to protect your child from an uncomfortable truth.

She made her choice: "Don't worry, you won't die," she said flatly. "Try not to think about it. Go back to sleep."

I did what she said. I went back to sleep — not just that night, but for years.

For almost a decade I completely forgot about that starry sky. Then, when I was in college, someone gave me a book, *Spiritual Gems*, letters written in the first part of the twentieth century by an Indian guru called the Great Master to disciples in America.

One of the first letters read:

Ascent

> During devotional practice, as the concentration improves, mind and soul vacate the body and pass through the eye centre, then cross the starry sky, the sun, and the moon, and meet the Radiant Form of the Master. From there onwards the Master's Form acts as a guide, and the journey is made in the company of the Master.

There it was:
> mind and soul vacate the body and pass through the eye centre, then *cross the starry sky* . . . .

Reading Great Master's description of an inner starry sky, I remembered how, in my bed, ten years earlier, I repeated "forever and forever..." to myself until I left my body and burst into a starry sky. I remembered running downstairs and telling my parents, "I don't wanna die." I remembered my mom telling me, "Try not to think about it."

Then I remembered forgetting all about it. There, a decade later, in college, I remembered the starry sky experience, long buried in the subconscious.

Spiritual Gems told me the ten year old boy's vision was real. And most exciting of all, it told me there were modern masters who could teach the method and technique so that the concentration achieved by that little boy, once on an uncontrolled impulse, could be developed, cultivated and experienced at will.

Yosemite Reverie

So in 1979 I took initiation from the Great Master's spiritual successor, Maharaji, who was living in India. Maharaji taught that there's an inner light and sound, a Creative Power flowing through us. He said it was called many names by many teachers: *Shabd* or *Nam* by the Sikh gurus of Northern India, *Kalma* in the Koran, *Tao* in Chinese philosophy, *Logos* or *Word* in the Bible. Maharaji called it *The Audible Life Stream* or *Sound Current*.

Meditation, Maharaji explained, is a "rehearsal to die," because just like at death, the attention is withdrawn from the body. But unlike the real death, the attention returns to the body at the end of the session. This is what Saint Paul meant, Maharaji explained, by "I die daily." If we practice dying in meditation every day, Maharaji said, we'll be ready when it comes. Death becomes a confident, smooth separation of soul from body, rather than a fearful, turbulent mess. He'd even titled his book on meditation *Die to Live*.

His meditation practice was very specific, practical.

It has three parts. The first, and most important in the beginning, is the silent, interior repetition of holy names given by the master at the time of initiation, also called *mantra* or *simran*. The mind is always thinking about something, always repeating thoughts, Maharaji said, and Repetition is designed to still the mind, focus it at the eye centre and help it remember its divine origin.

Ascent

In addition to the faculty of thinking, which is occupied by Repetition, the mind also has a faculty of seeing, which Maharaji taught us to occupy through Contemplation. A first we were to simply contemplate on the darkness within, to try to keep the attention in the darkness, to learn to love the darkness. Over time, as concentration improves and Repetition matures, we become aware of an inner light, Maharaji said, and ultimately we'd come into the presence of the Radiant Form of the Master. It appears as our master appears to us outside, talks to us and guides us on our journey. Contemplation is done at the same time as Repetition, so both faculties of the mind are occupied — the power to see by contemplation, and the power to think by repetition.

After doing Repetition and Contemplation for an extended time, Maharaji taught us to spend the last quarter or third of each sitting listening to the Sound Current — or, if the Current is not audible, to listen *for* it, to listen to the 'sound of silence.'

The Sound Current, he said, is the source of life, love, and joy. It's always ringing inside of us, though we are so unfocused and full of inner noise that we don't hear it. So the entire purpose of meditation is to still the mind so the soul develops its innate faculty to hear within.

Yosemite Reverie

At first we might hear nothing, or silence, but over time we'd develop our faculty of hearing and catch hold of the Current. It might be faint, like the tinkling of faraway bells, or the wind in the trees, or a distant train, but over time, as concentration improved, these preliminary sounds would develop into a sweet, strong, inner symphony.

This Sound Current he said, purifies the mind — and the soul, freed from association with the mind and body, rises on the Audible Life Stream towards its ultimate spiritual home. *Upwards flows the river,* wrote one Indian saint.

So from the day of Initiation, Maharaji and his teachings were the warp and woof of my life. Every day I'd get up and sit. Every week I'd go to *satsang* — meetings of our spiritual community. And whenever I could, I took the opportunity to travel to India or one of our Centers in the United States to be with my master, and enjoy his elevated company. He didn't have to say anything. Simply to look at him brought joy.

Through marriage, divorce, remarriage, births of children, deaths of family members, changes in jobs, houses, illness, health — meditation and satsang were the only constants. No matter what else was happening, no matter what changes I was going through, the tapestry of life was stitched with meditation and satsang, punctuated by the rare and wonderful days where I had the company of my master.

Ascent

I finished the tea, turned from the window, walked to the freezer and pulled out a frozen dinner. Next to the refrigerator was a calendar, with today's date circled. It was fortieth anniversary of my Initiation. "That would've been ironic," I said out loud to no-one, thinking how close I came to dying today.

Forty years on the Path. Almost fifteen thousand daily sittings. More than two thousand satsangs — each time hearing the same message, the same teachings.

After all that, was I ready? Was I ready to die?

I knew the answer. I wasn't. I hadn't rehearsed sufficiently. I'd been lazy, casual. I assumed I had plenty of time. If I had died today, I'm sure I would have blown it. I hadn't stilled my mind, I hadn't realized within.

Even after all this meditation, all these satsangs, I had no clue. Would my soul fly off to some starry sky? Or would it vanish into nothingness? Would I still be aware of myself? Would I meet the Radiant Form . . . merge into some beautiful ocean of love and harmony? Would "I" even exist?

These were no longer abstract concepts off in the far distance. It was urgent. It could have been today.

With the microwave ding another ding went off in my head: *go to the mountains, go to the mountains*. It had been too long. I needed clarity — peace — silence. By the time the enchilada was finished I had decided: *I'm going to the mountains*. I'm going

Yosemite Reverie

on retreat. I'm going to cut out all the noise, all the distractions. I'm going to break through!

I'm not coming back until I still my mind!

I remembered reading in another of Great Master's letters that if one were to hold the attention at the eye focus for three hours he must go inside. I was sure I could do that if I really worked at it, got to a quiet place and really tried. I would be on a quest. I was going to still my mind and go inside — and I was sure it wouldn't take more than a week.

So I sent a text to my assistant: "Gone for a few days, back next week. Personal time." He was used to my disappearances. It wouldn't phase him. I called my wife, visiting our daughter in LA, to say goodnight. I didn't tell her about my near miss. I just told her that since she was gone anyway, I thought I'd go to the mountains for a few days. "Follow your bliss," she said.

I took the dusty gear out of the closet, and spread it out on the floor: pack, tent, sleeping bag, stove, matches, water purifier, walking sticks, headlamp, boots. It was all there. I tested the critical items: counted tent stakes, blew up the thermarest — no leaks. Shook the gas canister — nearly full. Screwed it on the burner and lit the stove — works fine. Flushed water through the purifier — clean. Put fresh batteries in the headlamp and shined it on the wall. Check, check, check.

Ascent

Into the pack it all went. Then, into a small bag, the clothes: polar fleece layers, nylon slacks, several pairs of socks, down hoodie, wool watch cap. Filled four one-litre canteens with water, put them the bottom. Left a little room on top for food — get that later. Pulled it up by the straps and heaved it onto my shoulders.

"Uggh." Thirty five pounds, I guessed. Walked around the condo, felt it settle. Probably will be forty with the food. Heavy but manageable. Sat on the guest bed, slithered out of the straps, let the pack drop, left it there, and went to sleep.

Yosemite Reverie

3

I woke before dawn, heaved on the pack, rode the elevator down to the garage and got in the car. It rolled out onto empty streets and approached the Bay Bridge at the same corner where just twelve hours earlier I was nearly squashed like a bug.

The car mounted the span and carried me over the flat gray water, the sky lightening ahead of me. It didn't take long to blow through Oakland and enter the East Bay bedroom suburbs, watching the traffic in the other direction build, heading into the City. I stopped in Dublin, at the last Whole Foods, and stocked up: bread, cheese, a bag of tiny carrots, apples, trail mix, ramen noodle soup, tea, powdered coffee, dried fruit, instant oatmeal, mac 'n cheese, and, most important of all: dark chocolate covered almonds.

As I sped east, the sun rose higher and the temperature rose with it. At Manteca, I topped off the gas. The air was furnace hot.

Here I left the interstate and headed due east on Highway 120, a narrow two lane arrow pointed straight at Half Dome. By noon I was racing across the flat valley of Central California, piercing miles of endless almond orchards stretched for hundreds of acres on either side, tracing along a railroad track that serves large warehouses, food processing facilities and lumberyards piled high with long logs curing under sprinklers in the sun. Every few miles the road would cross over a branch of the California Aqueduct, a maze of trapezoidal concrete channels carrying Sierra water to ever-thirsty Southern California cities and farms.

After the last stoplight outside of Oakdale the highway begins to wind its way through the foothills, where open farmlands give way to oak savannah and digger pines. The road climbs slowly, through an undulating landscape, until, at about a thousand feet, it comes to the Don Pedro Reservoir, where the Tuolumne River is dammed, and the captured water backs up canyons and valleys to form a finger-shaped water body with an unnatural, jagged, steep shoreline.

Here the highway steepens and winds steadily past three thousand, four thousand feet, into the folded skirts of the Sierra. The gears downshifted and the engine purred without complaint. I opened the windows and let the wild in. Every few miles, on the passenger side, I heard small waterfalls leap and splash over large boulders. Every few seconds, an oncoming car flashed by the driver's side — *whoosh... whoosh, whoosh.*

Finally, I arrived at Big Oak Flat, about forty-five hundred feet above sea level, where a large sign announced: "Entering Yosemite National Park."

Yosemite Reverie

I stopped at the gatehouse and rolled down my window. A ranger in an olive green uniform wearing a stiff, broad, Smokey-the-Bear hat took my credit card, charged the entry fee, and gave it back to me with a park map.

"Welcome to Yosemite," she said.

"Yo-sem-i-tee," I said out loud to myself as I laid the map on the seat and drove on. I always loved the sound of that word. Yet "Yosemite" is one of the great examples of how mistranslation is perpetuated over time.

In the late 1890s, when the first white Americans entered the great valley floor, they asked their Miwok guides, "what's the name of this place?"

"Yos s e'meti," they answered.

But the Miwok, with their limited English, misunderstood the question. They thought the question was, "Who lives here?"

So they answered by describing the bandits and outlaws who hid in the walled valley in which they stood: *Yos s e'meti,* which means, "they're killers."

Many decades later, as Americans studied Miwok culture and language, they realized the name they gave the place we love has a profoundly different origin and meaning. Yet it persists, this euphonious name, only now it doesn't invoke fear of killers, but evokes images of peaceful meadows and towering granite cliffs with awe-inspiring waterfalls.

Ascent

I took the fork at Tioga Road, bypassed the famous Yosemite Valley floor crowded with tourists, and headed for the lonely high country.

The narrow road rose steeply, and the view opening and closing on the great granite landmarks along the winding way. After about an hour grind uphill I parked at the Tuolumne Meadows Visitor Center, opened the hatch, and sat on the rear deck. Immediately a sweater and watch cap — smell of pines and crisp air. It was now noon — five hours later, eight thousand feet higher, and much colder than where I'd started, at the edge of San Francisco Bay.

Yosemite Reverie

4

I kicked off my sneakers, left them in the back, and laced up my trusty boots — not the new lightweight mesh ones, but twenty-year old, leather high tops, with strong thick soles. These boots can take you anywhere.

I had no watch — it was broken, lying on my desk at home. I was going to get in tune with nature. I'd live by sunrise and moon set, not arbitrary numbers on a machine. I was on retreat. I was on a quest. I was going to still my mind.

I put the solar shade up inside the windshield, zipped the car key into the top pocket of the pack, heaved it onto my shoulders, grabbed my aluminum titanium-tipped walking sticks, shut the tailgate, locked the car, and started in.

As the trail climbed from the gravel parking lot into the woods, I began to notice the call of birds and the roar of wind through the branches in the tall steep woods. My breath began to find the rhythm of my stride. The pack settled on my shoulders.

Life became simple. Everything I needed was on my back, and I was alone with my thoughts. Deep in the granite folds

Ascent

I was blissfully out of range of any cell tower or wifi hotspot. After a couple of hours walk up an enclosed valley shaded by tall trees, the trail crested a ridge and opened up a long vista.

The entire panorama of the Sierra opened out before me. In all directions were the serrated snow-dusted peaks of the Range of Light. The Central Valley of California lay beyond the ridges, and the gentle Pacific was just out of view beyond the curvature of the earth.

On a geological scale the Sierra Nevada is young. When life is measured in decades, mountains seem solid. But measured in millions of years, rock is a stiff liquid — restless and always in motion.

The earth's land was originally one enormous mass geologists call "Pangea." About 175 million years ago Pangea began to break up into the continents we know today. These continental plates constantly move and grind against each other. They push up mountains, generate earthquakes, spew volcanoes, hurl tsunamis. And the mountains, in their turn, are ground by rain, glaciers and wind in an enormous cycle of freeze and thaw that breaks the largest boulders into countless grains of sand carried by rivers and dropped to form beaches which are in turn sculpted by crashing waves.

Seventy million years ago, the mass of granitic rock that's now the Sierra Nevada lay five miles thick and far below the

Yosemite Reverie

earth's surface. Around twenty million years ago pressure from the Pacific Plate, pushing eastward and northward deep below the North American Plate began to tilt this enormous block of granite upwards, ranging mountains along the entire continental margin — the Coast Ranges, the Cascades, the Tehachapi, the Sierra.

There, standing on top of that granite batholith, ever so slowly but inexorably being pushed up by the Pacific Plate, with rising mountains sending tremors up and down the spine of California, one life is an insignificant speck in space and moment in time.

This is why we ascend — you're on top of the world and profoundly humbled at the same time.

So what if I had died yesterday? Maharaji taught that the human form is unique and precious, because only human beings can become conscious of the divine. He said that after every life we're reincarnated into another body, one that reflects the actions and impulses of the life we've just lived. This cycle of birth and death continues for ages, and the soul is born and dies over and over, moving from body to body, trapped in a vast cycle of transmigration.

In Indian philosophy it's called *Charausi,* or The Wheel of Eighty Four, because the Indian saints say the soul incarnates through eighty-four hundred thousand different species before it gets a human birth. In the long scope of time, how many times had I been born and died already?

As Guru Arjun, the fifth Sikh guru, wrote five hundred years ago in a sacred hymn that's still sung today in villages across North India:
> In so many lives, you were a worm and an insect;
> in so many lives, you were an elephant, a fish and a deer.
> In so many— a bird and a snake.
> In so many— yoked as an ox and a horse.
> Now's the time— meet the Lord!

Was there any purpose to all of this birthing and dying? How many forms had I taken? How many times had I been a tree, holding on for dear life in the bitter cold wind and mining deep for water in the scorching hot sun? How many times a worm, burrowing blindly in the earth, mouth open, passing soil through myself, drawing life from fungus and bacteria? How many times a sparrow, restlessly searching for worms? How many times a raccoon, feasting in the dark on the eggs of sparrows?

Was there any point to this vast, eternal Wheel of life and death, of eating and being eaten?

The modern Zen philosopher Alan Watts wryly observed,
> There is a growing apprehension that existence is a rat-race in a trap: living organisms, including people, are merely tubes which put things in at one end and let them out at the other,

Yosemite Reverie

which both keeps them doing it and in the long run wears them out.

So to keep the farce going, the tubes find ways of making new tubes, which also put things in at one end and let them out at the other. At the input end they even develop ganglia of nerves called brains, with eyes and ears, so that they can more easily scrounge around for things to swallow. As and when they get enough to eat, they use up their surplus energy by wiggling in complicated patterns, making all sorts of noises by blowing air in and out of the input hole, and gathering together in groups to fight with other groups. In time, the tubes grow such an abundance of attached appliances that they are hardly recognizable as mere tubes, and they manage to do this in a staggering variety of forms . . . .

In satsang I had often heard how the soul breaks free of the Wheel and ascends, how it traverses regions of intense beauty on its way to heavenly realms. But here, standing on a ridge and staring across the slowly rising mountains I had to be honest with myself. I couldn't be sure about all that. I didn't know anything about heaven, or karma, or the soul. I had no experience other than this physical life — except the brief glimpse of the starry sky. In years of quiet meditation I had become more centered, more grounded, but I had to confess I still had no direct answers to the big questions, no confirmation for myself of the teachings that inspired me.

Ascent

I knew only two things for sure: first, I'd been born. Second — I'll die.

What's the difference between these two? It seemed to be the presence or absence of some animating power. When the power becomes active, matter begins to organize and grow itself into a living being, into living systems. When the power is withdrawn, the same matter which sustained life becomes inert and immediately begins to decay.

Call it consciousness, or soul, or attention. Maharaji taught that this is our true self. It's a flowing current of life that abounds within and surrounds without. "All you have to do," Maharaji taught, "is to focus your attention on the Creative Power and realize the Truth within."

That's the real me. Not this body, clearly, for the body changes, and in the end it dies. It nearly happened yesterday. Could happen today. Will certainly happen some tomorrow. This thing I call myself, this thing that looks out of these eyes and sees the landscape, that feels the breeze, that intends to walk or to stand, that thinks these thoughts — it's not the body, this wiggling tube. It's not even this personality I call myself — it's a particle of consciousness, a ray of the sun, a drop of the ocean.

That's the only escape: to transcend the body, lose the small self and realize the True Self, the Creative Power within — to merge the ray into the sun, the drop into the ocean. Yesterday,

Yosemite Reverie

on the street in downtown San Francisco, I saw how far I had to go. I was unprepared, unfocused, coasting along. Now, staring at the mountains spread out around me, revealing the shortness of life and the vastness of time, I realized — there's none to waste.

II. Glen Aulin

Yosemite Reverie

1

In this philosophical mood I followed the trail down from the ridge drawn by the sound of rushing water and made camp by the river just as the sun lowered in the west. Darkness falls fast in the thin mountain air.

At Glen Aulin campground the Tuolumne River cascades over large granite boulders, enjoying its brief freedom before imprisonment behind dams and tunnels to serve thirsty San Francisco. The air is cool and moist and delicious.

I dropped my pack at the base of an incense cedar, freed my feet from the boots and sweaty socks, walked to the river's edge and stepped in.

The water was near freezing — melted snow. The fatigue from the early morning drive and the long climb up the ridge drained into the fast flowing current. Knee deep in the roaring chill I splashed my face with ice water.

Behind me, I heard a voice:

"δὶς ἐς τὸν αὐτὸν ποταμὸν οὐκ ἄν ἐμβαίης."

Glen Aulin

I can't explain how, but I understood it: "You can't step into the same river twice."

I turned around to see an old man with a beard, wearing a rough cloth robe and leather sandals. Next to him was a small bundle and a heavy blanket.

It was hard to see the features of his face. They were obscured in the twilight, but I recognized what he had just said.

It was one of the most famous sayings of Herakleitos, an early Greek philosopher. He lived five hundred years before Christ, a hundred years before Sokrates, in Ephesus, on the coast of modern-day Turkey. His teachings, if they had ever been written, had been lost. What we have of his philosophy today exists only in small fragments and quotations by others.

Now Herakleitos sat on a rock next to my pack, under the cedar, speaking in ancient Greek as I was up to my knees in the Tuolumne River — and I understood every word.

"You?"

"Yes," he said.

"How is this possible?" I stammered.

"The river we step in is the same, and yet it is not the same, because we both exist and we also do not exist."

"No, not that," I said, "I mean how is it possible that you're Herakleitos, and I'm here talking to you!"

"Everything flows," he said, smiling, "and the river is always flowing by."

Yosemite Reverie

He gestured for me to sit. I squatted silently on the ground, dried my face with my handkerchief, leaned against the tree near my pack, and looked at him. Hard to believe, but an ancient Greek philosopher was sitting with me under an incense cedar, next to the Tuolumne River, high in the Yosemite.

Then, looking at his craggy, bearded, face, I saw a kind of shimmering golden light flickering in his pupils, like fire burning behind an isenglass window of an old wood stove. I was captivated, transported, by the light in his eyes. With it I felt something I had also felt when looking into master's eyes — indescribable love — love and acceptance unlike any other.

For a long silence we just looked at each other. He seemed to have a knowing smile on his face, like he was in on some kind of cosmic joke, and I hadn't yet been informed.

Then I realized how hungry I was. I hadn't eaten since I'd left San Francisco. I had packed everything, driven five hours, and walked six miles and climbed more than two thousand feet.

"Want some ramen noodle soup?"

He nodded, and said, smiling, "If happiness were in the pleasures of the body, we'd say that cows are happy when they find a bitter bush to eat."

I didn't know what to make of this comment, so I turned my attention to the pack: pulled out the cooking gear, screwed the burner to the compressed gas cylinder, rummaged in the food

Glen Aulin

bag for a couple of soup packets, ripped the packets open, poured everything into the small saucepan, filled it with water, put it on the ground, pulled a match from the waterproof metal canister, struck it, and sparked a flame. Cupping my hand to shield the wind, I held the match against the burner and opened the valve. The rushing gas leapt to life with an enormous sound. Then, carefully, I balanced the pot on the burner above the blue flame, held the handle and began to mix the soup powder, flavor packet, and noodles into the water.

All the while I was thinking what to make of the situation, sitting in the Glen Aulin campground of the Yosemite with Herakleitos in the flesh. He seemed to be only interested in philosophy, so I decided to make a go of it.

"I'm curious," I began, "My master says there's a Creative Power inside each of us. It can be seen as inner light and heard as inner sound. He says the reality of life is not the illusion we see all around us. He says the only truth is this One Creative Power, what he calls *The Audible Life Stream*.

"He also says that every mystic or saint who has looked within has experienced this Power, and they gave it different names. He says we start arguing about the names and lose sight of the real thing. It's like a thirsty man arguing about whether to drink *aqua, paani* or water.

He says the Greeks called this Power *Logos*. But the translators

Yosemite Reverie

don't understand this — they're intellectuals, they don't have a living master, they don't understand mysticism, so they translate *Logos* as Reason, or Account, or Reckoning. No offense to them — all translators bring their own perspective. When they translate *Logos* that way, it's impossible to get the esoteric meaning."

"Learning many things doesn't teach intelligence," Herakleitos said nodding his head in agreement. "Many divine things escape being understood because of disbelief."

"So," I asked, "What does *Logos* mean? Is there light and sound within?"

"The invisible harmony, is greater than anything visible," he said, "And thunderbolt steers all things."

He seemed to be confirming what a present-day spiritual master was teaching me. His teachings weren't some Eastern mysticism, or some new age religion. The teachings were the same, regardless of time, religion, culture, or language. Greek, Indian, Chinese, Persian — same.

"Although the *Logos* is universal — it's in everyone," Herakleitos said as if he could read my mind, "people live as if they have their own private understanding.

"For those who are awake, there is one Universe. But those who sleep each turn into their own private world.

"And regarding the *Logos*, which is eternal, people aren't able to understand before hearing it, or even after they've heard it once. And though everything comes into being through this *Logos*, they're unaware of its nature, even when I show them what it is.

"People just don't get it!" he said with a smile, "even when they've heard it. It's like they're deaf. We have a saying for it: 'present, yet absent.'"

"Yes, I think I get it," I said, "but sir, I'm frustrated. I've been meditating decades now... and still, nothing..." My voice trailed off. I was embarrassed and sad at the same time to admit it.

He seemed resigned, a little frustrated, like a teacher with a very slow student.

"The mix in the pot will separate if it's not stirred," he said.

I looked at the saucepan. The soup and noodles were fine. I had been slowly stirring it all along. What was he talking about?

Then I noticed he had been sitting absolutely still this whole time, just like my master would sit at satsang — motionless. He wasn't talking about noodle soup, he was talking about meditation.

He was making the point that we have to still the body before we can still the mind. He was saying that, like a mixture in a pot, if we don't keep stirring body and mind, the consciousness separates naturally.

It reminded me of Kabir's well known couplet: *thaan thir, maan thir.* "Still the body, still the mind."

Yosemite Reverie

I was beginning to see why, for thousands of years, he had the nickname "Herakleitos the Obscure." He never gave a straight answer. Only these little quips, riddles and non sequiturs. It was kind of zen.

"I guess I'm still fidgeting a lot," I admitted.

"I searched myself," he said, and then added, "The road up and the road down are the same."

He was, in his own obscure way, saying what all masters have said: we have to look inside ourselves, still the body and mind, and walk the Path by reversing the flow of attention. It's the same Path, the same road. Instead of going down and out, we have to go up and in. Today the attention is flowing out into the world through what master called the nine openings of the body — eyes, ears, mouth, nose, and so on. That's the road down. We have to reverse the flow of attention and follow the road up, to the "Tenth Door," the eye center, that leads within.

I divided the soup into two portions: half in the one metal cup I had with me and the other half left in the saucepan. I gave him the cup. Fortunately, I had an extra spork.

He slurped the broth and noodles.

"Is it OK?" I asked.

"Donkeys would rather have garbage than gold."

What could I say to that? He was always teaching, making a philosophical point, even in his jokes.

Glen Aulin

After a long day and strenuous climb, the soup really hit the spot, and I slurped it too, looking at Herakleitos. I thought about my near miss the previous day, and asked him, "What about death, sir? Is it final? I'm so afraid of being dead. I mean it's for forever... and forever... and forever. It's terrifying."

"Life and death are the same, sleeping and waking, youth and age... these change into those and those change into these, and back again."

"You mean death isn't the end?" I asked, "... just a transition into another kind of life?"

"A circle begins and ends at the same point."

"So it's a Wheel, like my master says, and the soul journeys from life after life in an endless cycle of birth and death, right?"

"Mortals are immortals and immortals are mortals."

"What?" I said, "what do you mean 'mortals are immortals and immortals are mortals?' That doesn't make any sense to me."

"Mortals are immortals and immortals are mortals," he repeated, "the one living the other's death and dying the other's life."

"You mean *karma*, transmigration, right?" I ventured, "the law that says we are stuck in a wheel of birth and rebirth according to our actions?"

He nodded.

"So, then what determines the next life?"

Yosemite Reverie

"A man's character is his destiny," he answered.

"You're saying our character — our actions in this life — determine our destiny in the next, right?"

He nodded again. He was a man of few words.

"It sounds so pointless," I said, "endlessly moving from death to rebirth, life after life. Is there a way out?"

"The bow is called 'life,' but the work is death," he said with smiling eyes.

He was making a pun. In Greek, the word for "bow" and the word for "life" are the same: βιός (*bios*). He was saying that this life is like a bow, and if we do the work of meditation, we can use this life to practice death, and propel ourselves towards our target — immortality.

Again he was talking about meditation. He was saying in his own epigrammatic way what my master always said — we need to use the opportunity of this life to escape from the Wheel by doing the work of meditation. "Die to live or live to die," he often would say.

"A man kindles a light within himself in the nighttime when his sight is extinguished," the Obscure Greek said. "In life he touches death when sleeping, and in sleep he awakens.

"Wait, wait, you're confusing me!" I said.

"Some people are unaware of what they do when they're awake, just as they forget what they do when they're asleep," he explained, "and death is what we see when we awaken," he said with

Glen Aulin

growing urgency, "all we see when we're sleeping is sleep!"

"I think I get it now," I said, "You mean if we wake up — if we find the light inside — not with these physical eyes, but with an inner seeing — we realize the truth about life and death. We experience death through meditation, we cross over to the other side, consciously and in our control, and awaken to truth."

He wasn't saying it directly, but in obscure sayings that would likely be incomprehensible to someone who hadn't been trained in meditation and the mystic way.

Yosemite Reverie

2

After we finished the soup I went down to the river and washed the pans. Then I climbed up to make camp. It was a clear, still night, so I decided to leave the tent packed and sleep under the stars. I blew up the thermarest, pulled my bag out of the stuff sack and fluffed it up, bagged the food and hoisted it in a tree on a long line — safe from hungry bears. Then I packed the cooking gear, leaving the stove, saucepan and cups out. All the time Herakleitos watched me quietly, lost in this thoughts.

"Cup of tea?" I asked. He nodded.

Again the strike of a match and the burst of blue flame in a loud roar. Again I held the saucepan carefully on the tines of the stove. At high elevation water takes a long time to boil. The sky darkened and began to fill with stars.

I poured two cups of hot ginger tea and handed one to Herakleitos. He pulled out a string of dried figs from his bundle and offered them to me. The temperature dropped quickly. We chewed on figs, sipped warmth and watched cold blue twinkling stars multiply and brighten.

Glen Aulin

We sat in silence for a while, the heat of the tea in the metal cups warming our hands against the night chill. I forgot about the improbability — the impossibility — of it all. I was just absorbed in being with him.

"Good and bad are the same thing," he said without any prompting. "To God all things are beautiful and good and just. But men have assumed some things to be just and others to be unjust."

"For example," he said, "sea water is both pure and poisonous. For the fishes it's pure — they can drink it and it gives them life — but for men it's poisonous — it they drink it, it's fatal.

"And it's not necessarily better that things turn out the way we want," he added with a chuckle.

"Disease makes us appreciate health, evil makes us appreciate good, hunger makes us appreciate abundance, and hard work makes us appreciate rest.

"God is day-night, winter-summer, war-peace, hunger-fullness. But he changes the way fire, when mixed with spices, is like incense — named after the fragrance of each spice."

"So you're saying these changes are just transitory? That life — God — is always changing his appearance, like incense on the wind?"

He sipped his tea without answering.

"I don't know," I confessed. "I don't see the divine in everything.

Yosemite Reverie

I keep making judgments. I get caught up in my needs, my desires, my fears. I've been meditating for years now and I haven't made any progress. It's just not working. I'm getting nowhere!"

He took a deep drink of tea, looked at the ground, and, after a long pause, looked at me and said, "If you don't expect the unexpected, you won't discover it — it's undiscoverable and trackless."

"You sound like Suzuki Roshi," I said to him, "You know, *Zen Mind, Beginner's Mind*?"

He gave me that empty, flickering, golden look.

"Suzuki Roshi says," I continued, "'We have to keep a beginner's mind... because in the beginner's mind are many possibilities; in the expert's mind there are few.'

"What you're saying, and what Suzuki Roshi says," I continued, "is that if we don't expect to make spiritual progress, if we don't keep a beginner's mind, we won't recognize progress even when it's happening.

We'll say, 'I've been sitting so long, I've done it so many times, I know what meditation is — it's just the same every day and nothing happens....' We're so full of judgment about our progress or lack of progress that we won't find the trackless track, we won't make the undiscoverable discovery.

"My master also used to tell us that to have success in meditation, we have to enter it with determination to explore its possibilities. He always encouraged us not to have reservations.

Glen Aulin

'Just be willing to go with it,' he said, 'do your meditation and let go.'

"I guess we get frustrated because we expect spirituality to be a certain way," I went on, "But you're saying — and my master is saying — it's not what we think it is. We have to let go of thinking we know what it's about, we have to expect the unexpected, we have to be open to the possibilities."

He smiled and nodded, "And you'll never discover the limits of the soul," he said, "even if you travel the whole Path, so deep is the *Logos*."

He was quiet for a long time. I was getting sleepy, and cold, so I fluffed my bag and crawled in.

"I'm sorry, sir," I said. "It's been a very long day. I can't keep my eyes open any more. I've really enjoyed listening to you. Can I hear more from you tomorrow?"

"οὐκ ἐμοῦ," he answered in the sweetest, most humble voice as he spread his blanket on the ground, "ἀλλὰ τοῦ λόγου ἀκούσαντας, ὁμολογεῖν σοφόν ἐστιν ἓν πάντα εἶναι."

"Not to me — but listening to the *Logos* — it's wise to agree that all things are One."

Yosemite Reverie

III. Ten Lakes

Ten Lakes

1

I opened my eyes before dawn, slithered out of the bag, walked down to the river guided by a headlamp, and dunked my head in the bracing water. *Everything flows*, I thought.

I came out and shook the cold water off, icicles running down my back, and my attention was drawn to the countless stars twinkling overhead in the cold, clear Sierra sky. My old friend Orion, with his loyal hound Sirius behind, were on their ageless journey through the fuzzy glow of what the ancients called the Milky Way, descending into the darkness behind the western ridge.

The ancients spent a lot of time looking at the stars, and they saw in their random patterns mythic characters engaged in battles, journey and quests. They imagined the fuzzy white band they saw in the sky was a path upon which these characters traveled — a Milky Way.

We now know that it's the edge of a disk shaped galaxy, and our Earth one small planet in a small solar system at the galaxy's outer edge. Imagine earth is a grain of clay in the outer rim of a

Yosemite Reverie

china saucer. Standing on this grain of clay we look through the saucer towards its center, where the tea cup sits, and we're looking deep into the galaxy's star packed center. Those countless stars, like grains of clay in a saucer, separated from each other by what seem like vast distances to us, are really very closely packed at the scale of space, so they make a blur of concentrated light which appears to us, here on earth, as a milky haze.

The ancients didn't know all that science. Yet, somehow, they understood these heavenly bodies move in graceful orderly procession, a sweet symphony. Pythagoras, one of the earliest known Greek philosophers called it *the music of the spheres*.

Was he talking only about the cosmos visible in the night sky? Or was it also some internal music, inaudible to the physical ear, but audible spiritually? Pythagoras, after all, had been accused by his detractors of "putting musical instruments into people's heads."

I remembered what Herakleitos had said the night before: "the invisible harmony is stronger than the visible one." And then, the last thing he said before I fell asleep, don't listen to me — listen to the *Logos*.

Were these ancients, in their references to an invisible harmony — a *Logos* that could be heard — talking about the Sound Current, the Audible Life Stream? Was all of life a divine vibration, and was that vibration audible to the spiritually adept?

Ten Lakes

Even modern physics is moving towards a theory that vibrating wave-particles are the fundamental building block of nature — string theory, they call it. Was realization nothing more than what an American philosopher called being "in tune with the Infinite"?

Walking from the river back to camp, I wondered did I really talk with the ancient Greek philosopher, Herakleitos? Did he really unroll a blanket and sleep near me?

I swept the area with the beam. No one. No blanket. Couldn't be. Must have been my imagination.

I fired up the little propane stove to make morning tea, boiled the water and poured it into my metal cup over a bag of PG Tips. As it steeped I saw something next to my pack: a string of dried figs.

I picked them up, examined them and pulled them off the string. There were only three left. I ate them one by one. They were chewy and sweet, with little crunchy seeds. They were definitely real — *but I didn't pack any figs.*

Then I remembered what Herakleitos had said: "If you do not expect the unexpected, you won't discover it."

I finished my tea, put the stove away, wiggled back into my sleeping bag, scooted up against the cedar tree, turned off the headlamp, set it on the ground, pulled my hood over my forehead as far as it would go and closed my eyes.

Yosemite Reverie

I began my meditation and looked inside, trying to "kindle a light within myself." I tried to imagine my master sitting there with me, in his spiritual presence, closer than my very breath. All the while the night's conversation with Herakleitos reverberated in my mind.

And though I had meditated every day for decades — almost fifteen thousand sittings — I tried to approach it anew, with a Beginner's Mind.

Maybe today I'll still my mind! Maybe today will be the breakthrough!

Maybe there were breakthroughs all the time, but I was so full of expectation or frustration that I didn't notice. . . .

Ten Lakes

2

I finished sitting as the birds began to twitter and the sky brightened. I washed at the river, ate breakfast, packed, and laced up my boots.

I decided to veer from the main path that followed the river downstream and instead climb the eastern slope of the ridge. It was only about eight miles and an eighteen hundred foot climb to Ten Lakes, a campground nestled in a granite plateau scattered with alpine lakes.

I walked silently, reflecting on last night's improbable encounter. From time to time the silence was punctured by the screech of a red tailed hawk. High above it played on an unseen force, first facing upwind, hovering, stationary, then banking, riding downwind under outstretched wings, swooping, cruising above the canyon.

In the late afternoon I approached the Ten Lakes campground. The elevation was near 10,000 feet, above the tree line, an undulating granite plateau with small alpine lakes sprouting in the low spots — bare earth, granite boulders, scrub junipers

Yosemite Reverie

and scree. It must be very hard karma to be incarnated as a juniper up here, pushing through rock for a toehold of nourishing soil, hanging on through centuries of freezing snow and dry cold winds.

I heard voices around the bend. The view opened onto group of men a few yards ahead standing in front of a large rock outcrop. They looked like Herakleitos: bearded, in rough loose robes and leather sandals, with blankets on their shoulders. I approached and asked one of them what was going on.

"The prison authorities have released Sokrates from his chains, and gave orders that he's to die today."

"Sokrates?" I asked. "Die today?"

"Yes," the man said, "Sokrates. You know him?"

"In a way," I said.

"I'm Phaedo," he said, greeting me. He was young, maybe in his twenties, thin, with a sensitive face.

He explained that Sokrates had been convicted and sentenced to death by the Athenian court for 'teaching false gods and corrupting the youth.' Instead of pleading for his life, or saying what the jury wanted to hear — he could have easily done that — they would have let him go — Phaedo said, he defended his actions. When he was found guilty, instead of taking the option of exile, he chose death, saying that we are wrong to think death is something bad, it's just a migration of the soul from one place to another.

Phaedo added that the execution had been delayed because of a religious festival, which ends at sundown.

"This is the day we've been dreading," he said. "When the sun goes down, he'll have to drink the poison."

Listening to this, and seeing the men gathering around the rock outcrop, I thought there must be some kind of warp in the fabric of spacetime.

Here I was in the Yosemite in the 21st century with Sokrates and his disciples. I remembered last night's talk with Herakleitos: If you don't expect the unexpected, you won't discover it. I had entered another world.

A stout, grey haired man walked out of the cave and sat on a large flat rock near the opening, blinking his eyes in the light, and rubbing his legs. He had wide set, bulging eyes, a flat, up-turned nose with flaring nostrils, and large fleshy lips. He was physically quite odd, but somehow also attractive.

"That's him," Phaedo whispered to me as the men gathered.

"How odd it is, friends," Sokrates said, " — this state men call 'pleasant,' and how curiously it's related to its supposed opposite, 'painful.' To think that the pair of them refuse to visit a man at the same time. But if anybody pursues one of them and catches it, he's always pretty well bound to catch the other one also, as if the two of them were attached to a single head.

Yosemite Reverie

"This is just what seems to be happening to me: there was pain in my leg because of the chains, and now, as I'm rubbing, pleasure has taken its place."

I sat on the ground next to the others. I must have looked very strange to them in my Gortex and fleece, but they didn't mind, offering a flurry of quiet introductions as Sokrates rubbed his legs: Cebes, Simmias, Apollodorus, Menexenus and others... the names came fast and I couldn't remember them all.

"I guess I'm off today," Sokrates said in a cheerful voice, "by Athenians' orders."

"How can you be so cheerful," one of the disciples asked, "at being put to death?"

"I'm not resentful," he answered, "but I'm hopeful there's something in store for those who've died — in fact as we've long been told, something far better for the good than for the wicked."

"Well then, Sokrates," said one of them, "will you keep your thoughts to yourself, or will you share them with us, too?"

"Yes, I guess it makes sense that someone who's about to make the journey to the next world should ask and wonder about what that journey is like — after all, what else should we do until the sun goes down?"

Ten Lakes

3

As Sokrates started to talk, another man, who looked older than the others, came out of the cave, and stood next to him.

"First let me hear what Crito wants," Sokrates said, "he wants to say something to me."

"Only this, Sokrates," Crito said, "the guard who's going to give you the poison has been telling me — he wants me to tell you — don't talk too much. Talking, he says, increases heat, and this might interfere with the poison. People who excite themselves sometimes have to take two or even three doses."

"Then," said Sokrates, "let him do his job and prepare two doses, or even three, if necessary."

"I knew you'd say that," replied Crito, "but he's been bugging me about it."

"Never mind him," Sokrates said, and then turned to us.

"Now with you for my jury I want to give my defense," he said, making a coy reference to his previous trial. "I'll show with what good reason, as it seems to me, a man who has truly spent his life in philosophy feels confident when about to die and is hopeful that, when he has died, he will win very great benefits in the other world.

"Other people are unaware that the true practice of philosophy is nothing other than practicing dying and being dead."

"Wait, what!?" I blurted out, surprised at my own lack of inhibition. The others looked at me.

"I learned in school that philosophy was a bunch of arguments and discourses — reasoning. You're saying philosophy is 'practicing dying and being dead.' That's very different from reasoning. You're saying the true practice of philosophy is the same as meditation, what my master called 'dying while living.'"

"Other people are unaware —" he repeated, looking at me without responding, "the true practice of philosophy is practicing dying and being dead."

"Now if this is true," he went on, "it would be very odd for them to be eager in their whole life for nothing but this, and then to be unhappy when it comes, the very thing they'd long been eager for and practiced."

One of the disciples laughed at this and said, "Sokrates, you've made me laugh, even though I wasn't feeling like laughing right now."

'Yes, Simmias," Sokrates said, calling him by his name, "let's talk about it: do we imagine that death is something?'

"Yes, of course," Simmias answered.

Ten Lakes

"And it's nothing but the separation of the soul from the body?" Sokrates asked. "And being dead is this: the body's having come to be apart, separated from the soul, alone by itself, and the soul's being apart, alone by itself, separated from the body? Death can't be anything else but that, can it?"

"No, it's just that," Simmias said.

And I added, surprising myself at how comfortable I was in Sokrates' company: "That's what Paramhansa Yogananda says, what my master says, too! Yogananda says that the object of all spiritual practice is to separate soul from matter. And my master, Maharaji, says that we separate the soul from the body in meditation as a preparation for death."

"Now look, my friends," Sokrates continued, talking to both of us, "and see if maybe you agree with me on these points, because through them I think we'll improve our knowledge of what we're examining.

"Do you think it's right for a philosophical man to be very interested in the so called pleasures of the body, for example, food and drink?"

"Not in the least, Sokrates," said Simmias.

"And what about sex?"

"No."

"And what about the other services to the body? Do you think a man like that values them? For instance, owning fancy clothes and shoes, and the other bodily ornaments— do you

Yosemite Reverie

think he values them, or does he avoid them, except as much as he absolutely has to?"

"I think the true philosopher avoids them," Simmias answered.

"Do you think in general, then, that such a man's concern is not for the body, but as much as he can stand aside from it, is directed towards the soul?"

"I do."

"Then it's clear the philosopher is different from other people because he releases his soul, as far as possible, from its relationship with the body?"

"It appears so."

"And it does seem that someone who cares nothing for the pleasures of the body runs pretty close to being dead."

"Yes, that's absolutely true!" I blurted out again, "Die to live!"

"And now, what about the actual gaining of wisdom?" Sokrates continued, "Doesn't the body limit us, if we partner with it in the quest? What I mean is this: is what we see and hear really true, or aren't the poets always harping on these themes, telling us that we don't hear or see anything accurately?

"Yes, of course," someone said.

"And yet if these of all the bodily senses aren't accurate or clear," Sokrates went on, "the others will hardly be so — because they are, surely, all inferior to seeing and hearing. Don't you think so?"

"Of course."

"So when does the soul attain the truth? Because obviously, whenever it tries to study anything in company with the body, the body completely obscures the search."

"That's true."

"So isn't it in deep contemplation, if anywhere at all, that it sees things as they really are?"

"Yes."

"And it contemplates best, I guess, whenever none of these things bothers it, not hearing or sight or pain, or any pleasure either, but whenever it comes to be alone by itself as far as possible, ignoring the body, and whenever, having the least possible association and contact with it, it strives for things as they really are."

"You're talking about meditation, contemplation, deep interior reflection," I broke in, feeling more and more a part of the group, "not just reasoning, which is what the translations I read in school all say.

"I never understood how the soul could see things as they really are through reasoning, especially since you've just said the soul can't rely on sight or hearing, which are the basis of intellectual reasoning. The truth always seemed to be beyond reason, beyond intellect.

Yosemite Reverie

"I understand that reasoning is a big part of what you teach," I added, "but I never understood, until now, that your practice includes something more — what you're calling deep contemplation, separating the soul from the body, practicing death, or 'dying while living.'"

Sokrates just looked at me, blinking. I'm not sure what he made of my reference to school, or translations. I'm not sure how he saw the time-warp we were in.

One of the others, I think his name was Alcibiades, broke in and said to me, "Let me tell you about something Sokrates once did. He started meditating on something at dawn one day, and stood there in contemplation. When it would not come before him, he wouldn't give it up, but stood there seeking. Soon it was midday, and the men noticed him — naturally they were rather surprised and began talking to each other about how Sokrates had been standing there since early morning in contemplation. And at last, toward nightfall, some of the Ionians brought out their bedding after supper — this was in summer, of course — partly because it was cooler in the open air, and partly to see whether he was going to stand there all night. Well, there he stood until morning, and at sunrise he said his prayers to Apollo and went away."

"What about *Logos*?" I asked, turning to Sokrates. "Herakleitos and some of the others talk about this *Logos*, the Word, but I haven't heard you say anything much about that."

Ten Lakes

"Writing," Sokrates said, "has this strange quality, and it's a lot like painting.

"The creatures of painting look like living beings, but if you ask them a question, they keep quiet. And so it is with words. You might think they spoke as if they had intelligence, but if you question them, wanting to know their meaning, they always say only one and the same thing.

"And every word — every logos —once it's written, is thrown around, both by those who understand and those don't, and it doesn't know who to speak to, or who not to speak to. When misused or wrongly rejected it always needs its father to help it — it has no power to protect or help itself.

"You're right about that," I said.

"So tell me, isn't there another kind of Word, another kind of *Logos* —," Sokrates asked, "which we see as the legitimate brother of this bastard one, both in the way it's fathered, and in its better and more dynamic nature?"

"What kind do you mean, and how is it born, as you say?"

"It's written in the soul of the student, and it's able to defend itself, and knows when to speak, and when to be quiet," he said.

"You mean the living and ensouled Word — the living and ensouled *Logos* of the One who knows — of which the written word is really just an image?" I asked.

"Exactly," Sokrates said.

Yosemite Reverie

Maybe now I understood why he didn't talk about *Logos* directly. He didn't trust words, he didn't want to be nailed down. He didn't want us to get lost in written words or writings about words. He was encouraging us to look for the living *Logos* within our soul.

Ten Lakes

4

The conversation was shattering all my preconceptions. The Sokrates in my schoolbooks was argumentative and intellectual. This Sokrates was saying true philosophy was the practice of dying and being dead — which was how my master described meditation — and that we see things as they really are, not with the physical eyes and ears, not through intellectual reasoning, but in deep thought or contemplation by separating the soul from the body.

"Sir?" I said, tentatively, "may I ask another question?"

Sokrates turned his penetrating, loving gaze on me, and waited for me to speak.

"I've always been afraid," I said, "even since I was a little boy, that when we die, when the soul's been separated from the body, as you say, it ceases to exist — it's just destroyed and it vanishes and we're dead forever and forever and forever.

"I'm terrified of dying. Forever is an unthinkable amount of time. But if the soul did exist somewhere," I continued, "gathered together alone by itself, and separated from the body, I'd have more hope and confidence.

Yosemite Reverie

"Can you reassure me, please? When someone dies, does his soul exist? Does it still have some power and wisdom?"

"Well," said Sokrates, smiling at me, "I really don't think anyone listening now, even if he were a comedian, would say that someone in my position is wasting his time, or is disinterested in the subject. So let's see.

"Now we have an ancient doctrine," he went on, "that souls exist in the land of the dead, entering that world from this one, and that they reenter this world and are born again from the dead.

"Now if that's true, if living people are born again from those who have died, surely our souls would have to exist in that world? Because they could hardly be born again, if they didn't already exist. So it would be enough evidence for the truth of these claims, if it really became plain that living people are born from the dead and from nowhere else."

"I guess so," I said.

"Let's see whether everything comes to be in this way: opposites come to be only from their opposites — for example, the beautiful is opposite, of course, to the ugly, just to unjust, and so on in countless other cases.

"So consider this: is it necessary that whatever has an opposite comes to be only from its opposite? For example, when a thing becomes larger, it must, surely, become larger from being smaller before?"

Ten Lakes

"Yes," I said.

"And again," Sokrates continued, "if it becomes smaller, it will become smaller later from being larger before?"

"Yes."

"And something weaker comes from something stronger, right? And faster from slower? And again, if a thing comes to be worse, it's from better, and if more just, from more unjust?"

"Yes, yes," I said, "I get it."

"Are we satisfied, then, that all things come to be in this way, opposite things from opposites?"

"Yes, yes," I said, trying not to show my impatience. He seemed to be going on and on about the same thing.

"Well then, is there an opposite to living, as sleeping is opposite to being awake?"

"Certainly," I said.

"What is it?"

"Being dead," I admitted.

"You say, don't you, that being dead is opposite to living?"

"I do."

"And that they come to be from each other?"

"Yes."

"Then what is it that comes to be from the living?"

"The dead."

"And what comes to be from the dead?"

Yosemite Reverie

"I've got to say it's the living."

"Then it's from the dead, my friend, that living things and living people are born?"

"Apparently."

"Then our souls do exist after we die."

"Yes, I guess so."

I was beginning to understand his method, going step-by-step in exquisite detail, looking at it from every angle, to build his argument. It was a fascinating experience, with Sokrates himself leading me one question at a time to see the obvious truth of the immortality of the soul, and lessening my fear.

Then he went even deeper.

"Now one of the processes here is obvious, isn't it? For dying is obvious enough, surely?"

"Yes," I said, "dying is obvious. We all die."

"So what to do?" he asked, "Shouldn't we assume the opposite process to balance it? Isn't it natural? Must we supply some process opposite to dying?

"We have to, I guess."

"What will this be?"

"Being born again — rebirth," I admitted.

"Then if there is such a thing as coming to life again, wouldn't this, coming to life again, be a process from dead to living people."

Ten Lakes

"Absolutely."

"In that way too, then, we're agreed that living people are born from the dead no less than dead people from the living; and we said that, if this were the case, it would be sufficient evidence that the souls of the dead must exist somewhere, from where they're reborn."

"Yes, sir," I said, "it makes sense from what we've just said."

Yosemite Reverie

5

I was so caught up in my conversation with Sokrates that I forgot about all the other men sitting around. They didn't seem to mind, so I asked another question.

"Sokrates, sir, you've said that the philosopher tries to separate the soul from the body, and that after death the soul exists in that other world, independent of the body. You've said it's then born again into another life.

"But if life and death are a circle, how do we escape? Do we just live and die and get born again, over and over, or is there a way out?"

He smiled at the question, then he said, "Suppose the soul separated in purity, detached from body, since it had no unnecessary relationship with it during life, but avoided it.

"Suppose also that it has been gathered together alone by itself — since it always practiced this — nothing other than the correct practice of philosophy, which is in fact the cultivation of dying without complaint, wouldn't this be the cultivation of death?"

Ten Lakes

"Yes," I said, "It's 'dying while living.'"

"If it's in that state," he continued, "then doesn't it depart to the invisible, which is similar to it, the divine and immortal and wise? And on arrival There, isn't it going to be happy, released from its wandering and stupidity, its fears and wild lusts, and all the other problems of the human condition, and, as is said of the initiated, doesn't it really pass the rest of time with gods?"

"Yes, that's exactly what my master told us, too," I said.

"But the soul which has been polluted, and is impure at the time of its departure, and is in love with and fascinated by the body and by the desires and pleasures of the body, until it thinks that nothing is real except what exists in the physical form — what can be touched and seen and tasted, and used for sex — the soul, I mean, accustomed to hate and fear and avoid what is hidden and invisible to the physical eyes, and can be attained only by philosophy — do you suppose that a soul like this will separate pure and unattached, alone by itself?"

"Impossible," I replied, "master always said 'we go where our attachments are.'"

Sokrates nodded in agreement, "And these souls — not of the good, but of the evil — wander around to pay the penalty of their previous evil way of life. And they continue to wander until they're finally imprisoned in another body, because the lust for the physical never leaves them. And we can suppose they find their prisons according to the natures of their previous lives."

"What do you mean, Sokrates, 'according to their natures'?" I asked.

"What I mean is that men who have spent their previous life in gluttony, and promiscuity, and drunkenness, and have had no thought of avoiding them, would pass into donkeys and animals of that sort. What do you think?"

"Yes," I agreed.

"And those who have chosen injustice, tyranny, and violence, will pass into wolves, or into hawks and kites. Can we imagine they'd go anywhere else?"

"Yes," I said, "with natures like that, absolutely. We're born into a body that reflects our behavior and patterns from the previous life."

"And there's no problem," he said, "in assigning to all of them places in line with their various natures and behaviors?"

"No, sir," I said, "No problem."

"Some are happier than others," Sokrates added, "and the happiest — both in themselves and in the place to which they go — are the ones who have practiced civil and social virtues like temperance and justice, which they acquire by habit and attention, but without philosophy and mindfulness."

"Why are they the happiest?"

Ten Lakes

"Because they'd be likely to pass into some gentle and social kind like their own nature, such as bees or wasps or ants, or back again into the human form, and we can say that good and moderate people come from them."

"Yes!" I exclaimed, "It's karma theory! Reincarnation! Transmigration! I always thought it was an 'Eastern' concept."

He smiled, and went on: "But no one who has not studied philosophy and who is not entirely pure at the time of his departure may enter the company of the Gods," he said, then after a long pause, "...only the philosopher, the lover of wisdom."

Yosemite Reverie

6

The conversation kept on for a long time. Sokrates looked at the question of the immortality of the soul, and its proper care, from every angle. One by one he satisfied each and every question — both mine and the others.

It reminded me of how my master would patiently engage in question and answer sessions with us, year after year, decade after decade, answering the same questions over and over, with love and patience, sometimes going back and forth with the same person for ten, twenty minutes at a time, until they were satisfied.

"Then it seems," he said, summing up, "when death attacks a person, his physical part dies. But the immortal part escapes death, departs and goes away whole and not destroyed.

"And, without a doubt soul is immortal and everlasting, and our souls really exist in that other world."

"You mean we're not dead forever and forever and forever?" I blurted out.

Sokrates looked out beyond us, beyond the small group sitting at the his feet. He seemed to be looking to the mountains and blue horizon in the distance, but at the same time he had an empty look —looking out but seeing within.

He came back to us and said, "Keep this in mind, gentlemen. If soul really is immortal, then it needs care, not only while this time we call 'life' lasts, but for the whole of time, and it would be extremely dangerous to fail to take care of it.

"Because if death was a separation from everything, it would be a godsend for the wicked when they died — to be separated from the body and from their own bad deeds that are bound together with their soul. But since the soul appears to be immortal, there's no way for it to escape from bad deeds or be saved except to become as good and wise as possible. Because the soul takes nothing into the next world except its education and training, and it's said that these are of greatest importance in helping or harming the newly dead at the beginning of the journey There."

Here I recognized a point that master repeatedly made to us: all the meditation, the way of life, the satsangs — all of it was focused on being prepared for the moment of death. He always said the moment of death was the inflection point that determined the direction of the soul's journey. If we had prepared during life, if we had lived according to our principles, what Sokrates would call a good and just and moral life, if we'd 'practiced dying and being dead,' then we'd die skillfully, escape our karmas, and the soul would be free to journey to its true home.

Yosemite Reverie

"Now it's said," Sokrates continued, "that when each man dies, the Guardian Spirit that was allotted to him during life leads him to a place where all those gathered must, after being judged, journey onward with a Guide whose job it is to lead them from this world to the next.

"And when they've gone through the things that they have to, and stayed there for the required time, another Guide brings them back here through many long cycles of time.

Here I remembered that first paragraph by Great Master that caught my eye all those years ago, where he confirmed the starry sky. In that letter he also told his disciple that the master inside acts as a guide, and the journey of the soul is made in the company of the master. Here Sokrates was also saying the soul has a guide within.

"Now the wise and well ordered soul follows along," he went on, "and is not unfamiliar with its surroundings, but the soul that's passionately attached to the body, as I said before, hovers around the dead body it's just left and the physical world for a long time, struggling and suffering a lot until it's led away by force and against its will by its appointed Guide.

"And if the soul is impure and has engaged in unjust killings, or other bad deeds like that, it arrives where the others have been taken, and everyone avoids it and turns away, and refuses to travel with it or be its Guide, and it wanders around by itself in a state of complete confusion, until, after a long time, it's taken forcibly to its proper dwelling place.

"But the soul that has passed through life with purity and moderation finds gods for traveling companions and guides, and each of them dwells in the place suited to it.

"Now there are many wondrous places on the earth, and the earth itself isn't the way those who are always talking about it believe it to be in size or in other ways, so someone has assured me."

"What do you mean, Sokrates?" asked Simmias, "I've heard a lot about the earth myself, but not this belief of yours. I'd really like to hear it."

"Really, Simmias," Sokrates said, "It doesn't take the skill of a great scientist to tell you about them, but to prove them— that takes more skill than even I have. And even if I knew how, I don't have enough time left to tell it.

But nothing is stopping me from telling you what I'm convinced is the true form of the earth and the places in it."

"That's good enough, I guess," Simmias said.

I noticed something about Sokrates style. It had an inherent humility: he always couched his main points in phrases like, 'as someone has assured me,' or 'I don't have the skill to explain. . . .'

It reminded me of how my master always transferred any knowledge or authority he had as coming from his own master,

Yosemite Reverie

and how he never asserted that he was in possession of an ultimate truth. He always made a suggestion, or gave a perspective, or explained from his own experience, emphasizing that we need our own experience to be sure of anything.

And with Sokrates, it seemed that when his language was most tentative, most humble, was when he was winding up to his main point, to his most important message.

So I leaned forward with great anticipation of what he would say next.

Ten Lakes

7

"Well then," Sokrates began, "this is what I believe. The earth is very large, and we live in a small part of it, living around the sea like ants or frogs live around a pond, and many other people live in different parts of it. Everywhere around the earth are many deep valleys of many kinds and shapes and sizes into which water and mist and air have collected.

"The earth itself is pure and lies in pure surroundings with the stars, which most of those who've studied these things call æther. The water and mist and air are the sediment of the æther and they always flow into these deep valleys, these hollows, of the earth.

"But we don't realize that we live in the hollows, but think we live on the upper surface of the earth, just as if someone who lives in the deep ocean would think he lived on the surface. Seeing the sun and stars through the water, he would think the sea was the sky, and because he's slow and weak, he has never reached the surface of the sea, or brought his head above water or come out of the sea to our region here, nor seen how much

Yosemite Reverie

purer and more beautiful it is than his own region, nor has he ever heard of it from anyone who has seen it.

"Our experience is the same. Living in the deep valley of the earth, we believe that we live upon its surface. The air we call the heavens, as if the stars made their way through it, this too is the same: because of our weakness and slowness we are not able to make our way to the upper limit of the air — if anyone came to it or reached it on wings and his head rose above it, then just as fish see things in our region when they jump up from the sea, he would see things There and, if his nature could withstand it enough to contemplate them, he would know that There is the true heaven, the true light, and the true earth.

"Because the earth here — these stones and the whole region — are spoiled and decay, just like things in the sea are by salt water. Nothing worth mentioning grows in the sea, nothing, we might say, is fully developed.

"There are caves and sand and endless slime and mud wherever it's mixed with earth — it doesn't compare in any way with the beauties of our place up here. Now in the same way, those things Above are in the same way far superior to the things we know. Really, Simmias, if this is the time to tell a story, it's worth hearing what things on the earth and beneath the heaven are really like."

"Yes, Sokrates," Simmias answered, "we'd love to hear this story."

Ten Lakes

I recognized this line of discussion. Sokrates had taken a simple physical example — geographical and astronomical theory — and turned it into a spiritual metaphor: the earth has high and low places, and we live in the lowest region thinking it to be the highest. We're like a fish underwater thinking this is the best place on earth. Raise your perspective, Sokrates was saying, using the fish jumping out of the water as his example, and break through to a more rarefied atmosphere, a higher level of consciousness. In fact, Great Master had gone so far as to say that to the spiritually enlightened, this world is a latrine!

"Well, my friend," Sokrates began, "the True Earth, when viewed from above, looks like those round balls made up of twelve pieces of leather. It's multicolored, divided into patches of various colors, like the colors painters use. There the whole earth is made of these colors, but much brighter and purer. One part is sea green and amazingly beautiful, one part is a marvelous purple, another golden, another white — whiter than chalk or snow. The earth is made up of other colors too, more numerous and beautiful than any we have seen.

"The deep valleys of the earth, full of water and air, gleaming among the variety of other colors, present a color of their own so that the whole looks like a continuum of variegated colors."

Sokrates wasn't talking about geography or astronomy anymore. This was strikingly similar to the descriptions of inner

Yosemite Reverie

chakras, or spinning wheels of color visible inside, that I've heard about in satsang, read about in books on meditation, and seen in mystical drawings. What he was describing as the True Earth, or ultimate abode of the soul, was not that different from how my master described the soul's journey towards its ultimate abode, which he called True Home, or *Sach Khand*.

"The trees and flowers and fruits grow on its surface with a similarly intense beauty, and also the hills and the stones, more beautiful in their smoothness and transparency and color. In fact, our rare, precious stones here — our carnelians, jaspers, emeralds and the rest — are mere fragments of those There. But all the stones There are like that — and even more beautiful.

"And the reason is that There they're pure, not eaten away or spoiled by decay and brine, or corroded by water and air which flow into the low points here and bring ugliness and disease upon earth, stones, animals and plants.

"The earth itself is adorned with all these things, and also with gold and silver and other metals plainly visible in rich veins in all parts of the earth so that to see them is a sight for the eyes of the blessed."

It didn't appear to me that Sokrates was telling a 'story.' He was describing a real place — a place he called There and Above. After proving that everything associated with the body — everything physical — is subject to decay and deception, he was now describing a place true, everlasting and free from decay.

Ten Lakes

Maharaji also always said that nothing subject to decay can be true. He called it *Maya*, Illusion. Truth can only be found in something that isn't subject to change, something eternal.

Sokrates was using the brightest, most colorful, most precious physical objects that his listeners would know — snow, chalk, gold, silver, carnelians, jaspers, emeralds, fruits — to describe a metaphysical reality brighter and more wondrous than the brightest and most wondrous things on earth.

They didn't have smart phones with retina display, LCD TVs, stained-glass windows, or electric lights. They lived in a world lit only by fire. During the day the brightest, most colorful things they would ever see were the colors of nature. They didn't even have fabrics with the bright colors of chemical dyes. It was a world of muted tones: browns and greys and blue-greens. Anything bright or colorful was fleeting — like a flower blossom, or rare — like a gemstone.

All mystics and saints are limited to the language of their listeners. They have to give examples that will resonate with the times. Here, Sokrates is using the most colorful, rarest things on this physical earth to describe what he called the True Earth — a place beyond the physical.

"There are many kinds of animals on it, and men also, some living inland, some at the edge of the air, as we live at the edge of the sea, and others live on islands surrounded by air close to

Yosemite Reverie

the mainland. In a word, as water and sea are to us, air is to them and the æther is to them what the air is to us.

"The climate is so good that people have no disease, and they live much longer than people do here. Their eyesight, hearing and intelligence and everything like that are as superior to ours as air is superior to water and æther to air in purity. They have groves and temples dedicated to the gods, where the gods actually live, and they communicate with them by speech and oracles and prophecies and by direct face-to-face conversation.

"They see the sun and moon and stars as they really are, and they are happy in all other ways."

If I hadn't been sitting on the ground I would have fallen off my chair.

This was exactly what I'd read in Great Master's letters from the early 20th century:

> During devotional practice, as the concentration improves, mind and soul vacate the body and pass through the eye centre, then cross the *starry sky, the sun, and the moon...*"

Could it be a coincidence: a modern spiritual master describing the inner journey in exactly the same terms as Sokrates? Scholars called Sokrates' description of the soul's journey a *myth*, a fantasy. But maybe it matched a modern master's description because they were describing a real place they had both experienced?

Ten Lakes

Sokrates was also answering a question I had been thinking about for a long time: if the starry sky was so beautiful, why was I so afraid, when, as a ten year old, I inadvertently burst into it?

Great Master explained, decades ago to another disciple, why the starry sky at first doesn't stay. He said that the soul might see stars and suns at "hit-and-miss times" like falling asleep, or when the mind is quiet, but can't stay there for lack of energy.

Sokrates was saying it's like a fish jumping out of the water and getting a glimpse of the earth above. The jumping fish doesn't have the capacity to sustain itself in that rarefied atmosphere — it gasps for air. Its "nature" can't withstand it — it's not prepared.

We don't believe fish can breathe out of water, and we don't believe the whole universe could be inside of us. From our experience as human beings we don't believe we can be divine.

But seeds buried in the ground become trees reaching for the sky. Water bound tadpoles become jumping frogs. Crawling caterpillars become floating butterflies. The seed, the tadpole, the caterpillar — they don't have to believe it's possible, they don't have to understand the science, they only have to be exposed to the right conditions and undergo the change.

Spirituality is natural. It follows natural laws. Regular, daily meditation is slipping into a cocoon, a chrysalis. Inside that cocoon, as we attune to *Logos*, we undergo the natural

Yosemite Reverie

metamorphosis from being human to being divine. We don't have to do anything, or believe anything. We only have to surrender to the process. It's natural.

The *Logos* does it. *Logos*, the creative power steering all things from within, as Sokrates would say, develops our nature. It enables us, over time, to breath and see and move in that True Earth, our True Home, that rarefied atmosphere — There.

Ten Lakes

8

After Sokrates described the happiness of people in the True Earth, he described regions There in detail — rivers and lakes and other places where souls gathered.

He was describing the journey of the soul.

Then he said, "When the newly dead arrive at the place to which the Spirit Guide brings each one, they first submit to judgment — both those who have lived honorable lives and those who haven't.

"Those who have lived an honorable life make their way to River of Woe, board ships provided for them, and journeying on these, reach a lake. There they live, and are purified by paying the penalty for any misdeeds they may have done. They're also rewarded for any good deeds, as each deserves.

"But all who are deemed incurable because of the enormity of their crimes, having committed many grave sacrilegious acts, or many wrongful and illegal killings, or any other deeds like that, their fate is to be hurled into the deepest hell — and they never come out again.

Yosemite Reverie

"Those, again, who're found guilty of curable but grave crimes, such as an act of violence in anger against a father or a mother, and have lived the rest of their lives in penitence, or who have committed murder in some other way, must fall into Hell, and when they have fallen and stayed there for a time, they are cast back again."

It was a horrifying description of crime and punishment, action and reaction, or karma. Then, he reached the conclusion of his 'story.'

"But as for those who are found to have lived exceptionally holy lives, they're freed and delivered from these regions of the earth, as from prison, and attain the pure higher region, and make their dwelling Above.

"And among these, those who have been adequately purified by philosophy live free of the body forever, and live in places more beautiful even than these, which it's not easy to reveal — and I don't have enough time anyway. . . .

"But it's for the sake of these things we've just told, Simmias, that we must do everything possible to take part in virtue and wisdom during life — for fair is the prize and great is the hope!

"Now to insist that things are just as I've told you wouldn't be right for a sensible man. But since our soul is evidently immortal, I think it's right for a man to risk believing — for the risk is noble — that either this, or something like it, is true about our souls and their dwelling places."

There goes Sokrates, again, I thought, undercutting his main point with humility.

"So one should repeat these things to oneself like an incantation," he added, "which is why I've prolonged this story."

Hearing him talk about an 'incantation' I wondered, was he referring to the practice of Repetition, or *mantra*, used to focus the mind?

Maharaji often said there were many ways to focus the attention at the eye center. Some focused on breathing. Some practiced austerities. Some stared at a point on a wall. Some observed silence. All of these were ways to focus at the eye center. But Repetition, Maharaji said, was the most effective.

Sokrates never talked about Repetition, or *mantra*, directly, but he did talk about "counting" as a key element of philosophy. I wondered if "counting" could be a shorthand for *mantra*, the way "sitting" can be a shorthand for the meditation practice — as in "do your sitting everyday."

Here, in his last moments, by talking about 'repeating these things... like an incantation,' maybe he was making an oblique reference understood by the initiates sitting with him. I wanted to ask but I dared not interrupt.

Yosemite Reverie

"For these reasons, then," he went on, "any man should have confidence for his own soul, who during his life has rejected the pleasures of the body and its ornamentation as being of no concern to him, thinking that they do more harm than good, but has seriously committed himself to the pleasures of learning, and hasn't adorned his soul with alien ornaments but with its true ornaments: moderation, righteousness, courage, freedom and truth — and in that state awaits his journey to the other world, whenever fate calls him.

"Now you, Simmias, Cebes — and all of you," he added throwing his penetrating look at me, "you'll make your journeys sometime in the future, but my fateful day calls me right now, as some tragic character in a drama might say, and it's about time for me to have my bath, for I think it's better to have it before I drink the poison and save the women the trouble of washing the corpse."

Crito, the senior-most disciple, stepped forward, and spoke solemnly, "Very well, Sokrates, do you want to leave any instructions with us about your children or anything else — anything we can do that would be of greatest service to you?"

"What I'm always telling you, Crito," he said, "and nothing new! If you take care of yourselves your actions will best serve me and mine and yourselves, too, even if you don't make any promises now.

Ten Lakes

"But if you neglect yourselves," Sokrates went on, "and aren't willing to live step by step, as it were, on the path marked out by our present and past discussions, you'll accomplish nothing, no matter how much or how eagerly you make promises now."

"Then we'll try hard to do as you say," Crito replied, "but tell us: how shall we bury you?"

"Any way you like," Sokrates answered without hesitation, "if you can catch me, and I don't get away from you!"

Then Sokrates added, waving his hand at his elder disciple, "I just can't persuade Crito that the Sokrates who is talking to you here and marshaling all these arguments is the real me. He thinks I'm the one he'll soon see lying as a corpse, and he asks how to bury me.

"And though I've been saying for some time and at great length that after I've drunk the poison I'll no longer be with you but will leave you to go and enjoy the good fortunes of the blessed, it seems that I've said all this to him in a vain attempt to reassure you and myself, too.

"Promise Crito on my behalf," he said, "the opposite promise he made to the jury. He pledged that I would stay and not flee, you must pledge that I will not stay after I die, but that I'll go away, so Crito can bear it more easily when he sees my body being burned or buried and he won't be upset on my behalf, as if something horrible was happening to me, and so that he won't

Yosemite Reverie

say at the funeral that he is laying out, or carrying to the grave, or burying, 'Sokrates.'

"For you know very well, my dear Crito, the misuse of words is not only bad in itself, but does real harm to the soul. No, have confidence, and say you are burying my body, and bury it any way you like, whatever you think proper."

Ten Lakes

9

After saying this he got up and went into the cave. Crito followed him. We waited. The disciples and friends of Sokrates were talking among themselves, saying how great a loss they were about to suffer, and reflecting on the conversation about the immortality of the soul and its journey homeward. They said they felt as if they were about to lose a father and would be orphaned for the rest of their lives.

It was close to sunset when they came back out. Sokrates sat on the big rock. The prison guard came and stood by him. He said to Sokrates, "Sir, during the time you've been here I have come to know you as the noblest, the gentlest and the best man who has ever come here. So now also, I know that you won't make trouble for me. You know what message I bring. Farewell. Try to bear the inevitable as well as you can."

Then he turned away, weeping.

"Fare you well also," Sokrates said, and, watching him go back inside, added, "we'll do as you ask."

Turning to us, he added, "How kind he is — this guard! During the whole time I've been here he's come in and talked

Yosemite Reverie

with me often — a very kind man. And how genuinely he weeps for me now.

"Come, Crito, let's do as he asks. Have someone bring the poison if it's ready. If not, have the man prepare it."

"But Sokrates," Crito responded, "I think I see the sun still shining on the mountains. It hasn't set yet. I know that others drink the poison a long time after they've received the order, eating well and drinking a lot, and some even enjoy intimate relations with their lovers. Don't be in a hurry — there's still time!"

"It's natural, Crito, for them to do that," said Sokrates, "for they think they'll get some benefit, but it's not right for me. I don't expect any benefit from drinking the poison a little later, except to become ridiculous in my own eyes for clinging to life, and to save it when there's none left. So please do as I ask and don't refuse me."

Crito nodded to a man who was standing near him. The man went into the cave and after a short time came back with another man who was to give the poison, carrying it ready-made in a clay cup. When Sokrates saw him he asked, "Well, my friend, you're an expert in this. What should I do?"

"Just drink it and walk around until your legs feel heavy, and then lie down, and it will act by itself."

He offered the cup to Sokrates, who took it cheerfully, without any tremor or any change of feature or color, but looking at

Ten Lakes

the man from under his eyebrows asked, "What do you say — can I pour a small libation from this drink to honor the gods? Is it OK?"

"We only mix as much as we think is necessary," said the man.

"I understand," Sokrates said, "but it's allowed — indeed it's a must — to say a prayer to the gods that the journey from here to There may be happy. This is my prayer. May it be so."

He brought the cup to his lips, and with no sign of distaste, drained it with one breath.

Until then most of us had been able to restrain ourselves. But when we saw that he was drinking — that he'd actually drunk it — we burst into tears. Phaedo buried his face in his hands, sobbing. Crito had moved away, unable to hold back. And Apollodorus, who had been sniffling and crying the whole time, exploded into such a storm of weeping and wailing that everyone broke down except Sokrates himself.

"What strange behavior, gentlemen!" he said. "It was mainly for this reason that I sent the women away, that they wouldn't make this kind of scene. In fact, it's said that one should die in silence. Calm down, now, show some strength."

With this, we became quiet, ashamed. He walked around, and when he said that his legs felt heavy he laid on his back on the big rock. The man — the one who'd administered the poison — felt him, and after a while examined his feet and legs. He

Yosemite Reverie

pinched his foot hard and asked if he could feel it, and Sokrates said, 'no.' After that he felt his shins again, and moving upwards along his torso like that, he showed us that Sokrates was becoming cold and numb. The man went on feeling his body and said that when the coldness reached his heart, he would be gone.

I realized in that moment that Sokrates was showing us how to die. He was demonstrating the exact same process of withdrawal of the attention from the body that is practiced during meditation — except in meditation the connection with the body is not severed, the practitioner can return.

By the time the coldness was somewhere near his belly, when he uncovered his face — he had covered it — he spoke: "Crito — we owe a cock to Aesclepius: please pay the debt, and don't forget!"

Here, even at the very last, Sokrates was making a point, a joke. It was custom to give a sacrifice to the God Aesclepius as payment for healing an illness. Sokrates was saying that life is the disease and death is the cure.

"It will be done," said Crito, "is there anything else?"

No answer.

After a moment Sokrates' body twitched a little. Then his eyes became fixed, his body still. Crito stepped forward and closed his mouth and eyes.

Ten Lakes

He was gone.

It came flooding over me — that early morning phone call in June 1990. The voice at the other end, calling from India, told me that Maharaji had left us — a loss too enormous to bear.

Now, in this granite cathedral, watching Sokrates so willingly depart, I felt again the pain of being orphaned, of losing the best and wisest friend I had ever had.

I got up and walked briskly away from the group, shaking in grief, sobbing. They, also, were struggling with their emotions, clustering around the body — not around Sokrates — he had escaped — but around the body that had brought so much love, and wisdom and joy to their lives. My master had died naturally, at least. Theirs had been taken from them in the prime of life by an unjust trial.

I went down to the lake and plunged my head into the cold water to stop the sobbing. I wiped my face with my sleeve and let the cold water drip from my hair down my back and shoulders. For a long time I sat on the shore, looking at the trees and ridges reflected on the still surface in the purple twilight.

As the sky darkened I slowly got up from the lake shore and walked back. Was it all a dream? I wondered. Is it possible that I really was present at Sokrates' last dialogue, his last *satsang*? No, it had to have been my imagination. I approached the cave — empty, no one. Just my backpack on the ground.

Yosemite Reverie

I got out my headlamp, turned it on, and peered into the cave. The beam swept its walls. I walked in a few paces — only a few feet to the back wall. Nobody there. Just the nest of some animal on the ground in the corner. Leaves, sticks, scat.

Just a dream. Impossible.

Sokrates died twenty-four hundred years ago. No way I could have seen him here, met Phaedo, Crito and the others, heard him describe the true practice of philosophy as 'practicing dying and being dead,' no way I could have been present at his description of meditation as the soul's separating itself from the body as far as possible, no way I could have talked with him the way I did with my own living master, no way heard him describe so beautifully the inner journey of the soul, seeing the 'sun and moon and stars as they really are.' It's not possible that he drank the poison, and withdrew his attention from his body so skillfully and painlessly, without fear or trepidation, here on this rock outcrop in the Yosemite.

But wait — what's that? On the rock, nestled in a crevice: a few shards from a small handmade ceramic cup. I brought one to my nose: a bitter, acrid smell. How to explain it? Like Herakleitos and his figs, it was impossible, yet here it was.

It was getting dark — and cold. The sun had been down for I don't know how long — about half an hour? I unrolled my

Ten Lakes

Thermarest, unstuffed my sleeping bag and laid on the ground near the rock at the entrance to the cave.

    I thought about eating and setting up camp, but I was exhausted, drained. I'll just lie down for a few minutes first, I thought, the events of the day running through my mind.

IV. Bhog Joonni

Bhog Jooni

1

I woke to grunts and a musty smell — opened my eyes, head sideways, and saw a large fuzzy black shape silhouetted against the starry sky.

The shape was moving, making noises. Gradually, my sleeping consciousness reentered my body and I became aware of my surroundings. It was a California black bear — *Ursus americana californiensis*. She had her backside towards me, not more than a few yards away, so close I could smell her musty fur.

Uh-oh, I thought.

Bears are not uncommon in the Sierra. They're shy. They keep to themselves. If they show themselves to you, it's a great privilege and an opportunity. If you keep a distance, and don't make sudden moves, the bear will give you a look and move on. The Native Americans believe that each animal carries a special power, or blessing, they bestow on a person through association — they call it "animal medicine."

But to get that medicine requires a certain decorum. It's not our home. It's theirs. And the first rule is not to tempt them with

Yosemite Reverie

food. That's why before anyone goes to sleep in the high Sierra they hang their food high in a tree branch on a long line or stow it in a bear proof container. Otherwise, the bear will come at night and rut through your stuff.

It's bad for the bears — they get used to human food. And it can be catastrophic for the human. If you startle them while they're eating your food they can turn on you.

After the mind-blowing encounter at Sokrates's last dialogue, I had fallen asleep, exhausted. I forgot to hang my pack. Now a bear — no, there's another shape — it's two bears — two bears are rutting through my stuff just a few feet away.

I tried to assess the situation. I was in the open, zipped into a sleeping bag. Couldn't run, couldn't move. They certainly knew I was there, and they had their backs to me. If I did anything to startle them, there's no telling what might happen.

So I decided to talk to them.

"Hello, Mr. & Mrs. Bear," I said. "Hello."

The grunts stopped. They faced away from me, motionless. I saw their ears twitching, listening.

"Hello, Mr. Bear, hello, Mrs. Bear," I said again, as cheerfully as I could.

"I'm right here. I won't hurt you. Hello."

They turned their large bodies towards me, looking. I saw the light of the moon, low in the west, reflected in two pairs of eyes.

Bhog Jooni

I could hear them breathing. They stood next to my pack, having zipped open the pockets and spread out food and gear around them. Yes, bears in the Sierra know how to unzip a zipper. I had seen it on a Be Bear Aware video in the Ranger's Station. Now I was seeing it live.

"I'm sitting up now," I said, gingerly, as I wiggled out of my bag. "Is that OK?"

They just kept looking, so I sat up and turned to them.

"I won't hurt you, I'm a vegetarian," I said, realizing as the words came out how stupid it must sound.

Then, one of them took a step towards me. I froze.

"We don't want to hurt you, either," she said. "We're just hungry, and we found your food lying here."

I blinked my eyes. It was strange enough that I was talking to the bear. Now the bear was talking me.

"We've had so many dry years up here," she went on, "and it's hard to find berries. We're always hungry these days. We really need food."

"You can take it, I don't mind," I said, voice quaking. "Please just don't hurt me."

"Oh, we don't want to hurt you," the other one said, "We just need to eat."

"Good," I said, "Eat. Eat as much as you want."

I watched them for a few minutes, munching and pawing through my stuff. We were in an intimate trans-species

Yosemite Reverie

communion — together, alive, in the dark, just breathing together, alert.

They weren't sure if I would attack them, and I wasn't sure if they would attack me. The presence of imminent death and danger makes everything more vivid. There's no time to worry about the future or fret about the past. I guess that's why people jump from bridges on bungee cords, or climb El Capitan, or free fall from planes — to be forced into the moment, into the present.

I twisted in my bag to see them better. I didn't realize it, but my aluminum walking sticks were leaning against a rock near my feet. The bottom of the bag brushed against one of the sticks and they both crashed to the ground, clanging against each other.

Startled by the noise, one of the bears snapped. She charged.

Instinctively, I folded my arms over my head and ducked. Hot breath against skin. I rolled from my bag and wiggled out, tossing off the bear. Scrambling to stand up I felt one of the walking sticks on the ground. The bear was standing on her hind legs in attack posture. I took the stick, stood up, swung it around, and whacked her on the side of the head.

Then I poked as hard as I could into her chest. Her thick fur blunted the lunge. But she stopped in her tracks and let out a wild, guttural shriek.

I also shrieked: "You said you wouldn't hurt me!"

Bhog Jooni

We stood glaring at each other, me waving the stick at her, she now down in a crouching posture, nostrils flared, hackles bristling, eyes aflame, ears back. Gone was the congenial face that transcended her nature and held me in conversation. There was no hint of communion or sympathy. She was all instinct, all animal, ready to attack.

The masters teach that only humans have choices. Animals don't — they act only from instinct. Animals are *bhog joonni*, meaning just going through their life. Humans are *karam joonni*, meaning making choices, taking actions.

Animals can't choose. They can't create karma — they only go through it on their evolution to higher levels of consciousness. She heard a noise, got startled, and attacked. She had no choice. Pure instinct. Every fiber of her being was now tense, her blood pulsing with hormones, her muscles tightening. Once frightened she had no choice — she attacked. By all indications she was preparing to attack again.

Only humans have choice. Make right choices — realize the human potential. Make wrong choices — pay the price.

Then I noticed blood on my clothes and became aware of a throbbing pain in my arm. She had torn a gash when I had buried my head in my arms. There was no telling if she would lunge again. This was no time for philosophy.

So I made a choice.

Yosemite Reverie

Barefoot, in sweatpants and sweatshirt, with nothing but a single aluminum, titanium-tipped walking stick, I turned into the dark, and ran.

Bhog Jooni

2

At first I felt the pain of bare feet pounding the ground. But it receded into the background against the overwhelming fear of the bears.

I ran and ran. It was pitch black, the moon had set. . . couldn't see. No idea what direction I was running, or where the trail was. . . just ran into the darkness, holding my uncut arm in front of my face to protect it from high branches. Every few strides my foot would come against a boulder or log and it took all my effort not to stumble crashing to the ground. Somewhere the walking stick fell out of my hands and I didn't dare stop to look for it.

After several minutes running I stopped and tried to be as still as I could be. Didn't hear anything. The bears hadn't followed. They were probably back at camp eating.

I had bolted from the campground through the brush. I had no idea which direction I had gone. Was sure it was generally downhill, into the brush. Now I stood in the deep dark of the wilderness with no map, no GPS, no flashlight, no shoes, no

Yosemite Reverie

clothes except a sweatshirt and pants. Couldn't risk walking into a dead end canyon — I might never come out.

I looked up for the Pole Star or a constellation to get my bearings. If I could at least find north, I could maybe make my way east towards the river, and then trace it back to the car. But clouds had rolled in. No stars. Thunder rumbled across the distant granite peaks and leaves began to swirl in the wind. Mountains make their own weather — a crystal clear day can turn into a howling night.

I stood as still as I could, straining to tune in, get a sense of direction, find the path.

After a few minutes, I thought I could make out blue-black patches of sky in gaps between the rolling clouds. That had to be east. I took a few steps, tentatively, towards the light and picked my way carefully in the dark through the brush and branches. Again a rumble of thunder ricocheting across the granite walls. After a few minutes a light rain on my face.

In no time a downpour. My cotton sweats were quickly drenched with cold cold wet. I was already at eight thousand feet elevation and the rain was falling from clouds high above — the drops near freezing. Even some hail. The faint hint of dawn was obscured by thick clouds. I was blind in the woods.

A flash of lighting followed closely by a strong crack of thunder — the storm now directly overhead. Again a flash and a rumble.

Bhog Jooni

A few seconds later I heard the tumble of rockfall reverberate in the distance — the storm had made its contribution to the eternal shaping of the canyons and cliffs.

The situation was becoming serious. I kept moving, looking for a large tree to shelter under, or, better, maybe a small cave or rock outcrop where I could ride out the storm and wait for dawn. I just tried to focus — put one foot in front of the other. Then, without warning, I heard a crack, a slicing pain shot up my leg, and I fell to the ground, hitting my head on a rock.

I balled up, clutching my ankle, writhing in pain. It took a full minute to catch my breath, and collect myself.

Still on the ground, still clutching my ankle, I tried to assess: I was lying at the base of an enormous rock. I'd walked right into it and twisted my ankle, and, coming down, hit my head on it. I tried to stand, but the ankle couldn't bear weight. I could taste blood coming from my forehead. I reached up to feel a gash.

I was completely exposed, shivering, in the dark rain, bleeding from the arm and head, unable to walk, with lighting and thunder exploding and rolling all around me.

I slithered closer towards the rock and stretched my arms up and to the sides. It was taller than I was — how much taller I couldn't tell. I crawled along its base — it went on for several feet . . . wider than a small house. After crawling a few feet my nose came into contact with the buttressed roots of a large Jeffrey

Yosemite Reverie

Pine that had planted itself at what seemed to be the end of the rock. The distinctive vanilla fragrance of the bark soothed my nerves. I lay there for a few moments feeling the tree's presence, breathing and sucking moisture from the soft sweet mossy furrows. Even though I was drenched outside from the rain, I was thirsty from running — I hadn't drunk anything since the night before.

After a few moments I realized an overhanging ledge, just above, projected about three feet from the rock face. The ledge, together with the branches of the tree, provided a little shelter. Feeling the ground, I discovered a small pile of leaves and branches that had been swept over time under the ledge by the wind.

I scratched into the leaf pile — dry soil. The cotton sweats dripping cold, hanging heavy on my body, were draining the life out of me. I slithered out, and cast them aside, and naked, covered as much of myself as I could in the pile of leaves. I curled into the fetal position, closed my eyes, drawing warmth reflected off the leaves back into my body.

The storm kept getting stronger.

In the dark I became keenly aware of sounds. The driving rain, rising and falling in intensity with the storm, the wind whipping through the trees, and the trees creaking and groaning, the thunder rolling and cracking above, and the intimate

Bhog Jooni

sounds of drops falling from the ledge above and landing on the ground in front of me.

Had I ever paid this much attention to the sound within? For years I'd been complaining that I wasn't hearing anything. But what if it was there the whole time, maybe like rain in the distance, as master said, or wind in the trees — but I wasn't paying attention? What if I was so preoccupied with watching the clock — *is the time up yet?* Or evaluating what was happening — *why don't I hear anything?* Was I like those hapless people Herakleitos described the other night, unable to understand *Logos* before hearing it, or even after they've heard it....?

I began Repetition. This wasn't the usual slow unfocused repetition I had done in all those ambling meditation sessions — it was Repetition as if my life depended on it. I realized I should have been practicing with this same intensity all along. I'd heard so many times meditation was a rehearsal to die. Now I could feel death breathing next to me, waiting.

I remembered that Russian pilgrim, who, crossing Siberia on foot through ice and snow, was able to generate warmth by ceaseless interior prayer. He repeated *Lord Jesus Christ have mercy on my soul*... tens of thousands of times a day until it fully occupied his consciousness and enabled him to overcome freezing cold, deep hunger, and all kinds of illness.

Yosemite Reverie

I fought to keep the words rolling, to keep my fears and thoughts at bay, but I was failing. Will I die here — naked on the ground like a stray dog? This isn't how I imagined it. Where's my family huddled around me? Where's the white light and the symphony of music? *Where's my master!?*

My biggest fear was falling asleep. If I fall asleep, I thought, I'll never wake up. Naked, half buried in leaf litter, under the poor shelter of an overhanging rock, thunder rolling above and shaking the ground below, flashes of lighting exploding the blackness, in the roar of driving rain, I struggled with one thought: *I'm not ready!*

V. Smith Peak

Yosemite Reverie

1

I became vaguely aware of an otherworldly melody, with harmonies drifting in and out. Gradually, as my consciousness collected itself, I began to make out a pattern. It was a choir of heavenly voices repeating the same lines over and over, but I could not make out any words. It was some kind of language vaguely familiar, yet foreign — transfixing, transcendent, sublime.

I tried to shift towards the melody, towards the voices weaving in and out, towards the music pulling me, but couldn't move, couldn't feel my body. Am I dead? Am I in heaven?

I felt heat and light on my face. I opened my eyes. I wasn't dead. I was wrapped in warm, rough blankets, lying on a bed of pine branches, on my side, with a long view across a broad valley and serrated range in the distance. The storm had passed. It was a clear glorious Sierra morning.

With effort I rolled to face the other direction. I could see I was at Smith Peak, a mountain campground only a few miles from Ten Lakes, where I'd left camp and ran from the bears. I'd

Smith Peak

been at Smith Peak before, a few years ago, and recognized the bald round summit and the campsites arrayed in an arc looking out in all directions.

My attention was still drawn to the heavenly music. I saw nearby, at one of the campsites, a group of ten or twenty men and women stood in a circle, singing. They wore long robes of rough woven fabric and leather sandals. Nearby lay bundles tied together with rough rope and wooden staffs. They looked like they came out of another time — no fleece, no bright colors, no nylon, no technical boots. These were not ordinary backpackers.

They kept repeating the hymn, in an ethereal melody that sounded Persian or middle-eastern. I began to recognize it — the Prologue from the *Gospel According to John* in the original Greek:

Ἐν ἀρχῇ ἦν ὁ λόγος,
καὶ ὁ λόγος ἦν πρὸς τὸν θεόν,
καὶ θεὸς ἦν ὁ λόγος...

In the beginning was the *Logos*,
and the *Logos* was with God,
and the *Logos* was God.

It was present with God in the beginning.
Through It all things came into being,
and apart from It not a thing came to be,
That which had come to be in It was life,
and this life was the light of men.

Yosemite Reverie

They sang these poetic lines over and over, building themselves into an ecstatic trance. I tried to move and immediately felt a sharp pain in my arm, head and leg. Then the memory of bears, running in the dark, flashes of lightning, rumble of thunder, rain, cold and a crippling crash into a boulder.

I lay there transfixed, watching, listening. The pain vanished. I was no longer aware of my body. I was only aware of their singing, swaying, eyes closed, voices weaving in and out of harmony.

It was *kirtan*, the congregational singing of scripture. I had often lost myself in Maharaji's satsang, listening to hundreds of thousands of voices raised together, flowing in and out of spontaneous, ethereal harmonies, singing the sacred hymns of Northern India.

Not even a heart of stone can resist this outpouring of human emotion and love. Human voices raised together in longing for the divine are perhaps the closest external experience to hearing the sound within. Maybe that's why congregational singing is found in almost every religious tradition.

As I listened to them sing, I realized they were singing praises to *Logos* — the Creative Power, not to a particular person.

In the beginning was the *Logos*, they sang. *It* was the life and the light of men. Through *It* all things were created. Apart from *It* nothing came to be. Whatever came to be in *It* was life itself.

Smith Peak

For centuries, these lines have been interpreted as referring to the person of Jesus. "He" was the light and life of men, through "him" all things were created. But the original Greek is ambiguous: it can be either gender: male or neuter. "He" or "It."

Here, in context, listening to them, I realized that this *Logos* they praised was not Jesus the man — the embodied *Logos* — but the *Logos* itself, the Creative Power, conscious and alive, permeating all things.

Yosemite Reverie

2

After a few minutes they stopped singing. A young woman turned and saw me. She was thin, delicate, wearing a hooded robe that covered her flowing brown hair, and moved gracefully towards me.

"Brother," she asked, "are you alright?"

The spell broke. Pain, thirst and hunger flooded back. I became aware again of my body. She bent down and unwrapped the shroud, looked carefully at my sweat and blood encrusted arm, and then at my feet, blood coming through the cloth.

"You're bleeding, you've been hurt" she said. "Here, here, have a seat."

She helped me stand. I realized I had been not only wrapped in a shroud of some kind, but also dressed in a robe. I was weak and unsteady. She motioned two men standing nearby to help me. They placed my arms around their shoulders and helped me hobble to a large rock and covered it with a thick blanket.

Gently, gracefully, they set me down. She picked up a clay

pitcher and cup and poured a dark red drink. With both hands I raised the cup to my lips and drank it in one go.

"Wow, that's good," I said. "Thank you," I added, wiping my lips.

"You're welcome," she said, and refilled the cup.

Again in one go I drank it all.

Now she reached into a basket next to the pitcher and pulled out a loaf of brown bread, tore off a piece and held her hand out.

"Thank you," I said, wolfing it down, "Thank you."

"You're most welcome," she said again. I looked into her eyes and saw a serenity and love that was strangely familiar and yet completely new at the same time.

The two men sat silently next to me. As I ate and drank I began to realize how dehydrated and exposed I had been. I began shaking in the cool mountain breeze.

She wrapped a blanket around my shoulders. Then she knelt down and unwrapped my feet, exposing cuts and bruises.

"What happened?" I asked. She explained that they had found me unconscious, under a rock, not far from camp, while out for a morning walk after the storm. They carried me up to their mountain-top camp, wrapped me in a shroud, and lay me on a bed of pine branches, praying for my recovery.

I told them I had been attacked by a bear. I didn't mention that she talked to me first, or about the conversation with

Yosemite Reverie

Sokrates the day before, or Herakleitos the night before that — who would believe me, anyway?

"You've been through an ordeal," she said, "let us help you. I'm Mary Magdala."

She wiped the caked blood from my arm and head with a moist cloth. I winced. She poured water on my wounds, flushing out the dirt, then took some poultice from a jar and patted it on my head, arm and feet. Something herbal, I guessed, soothing. She began to carefully bandage my arm.

"And I'm Thomas," said the one of the men. He was stoutly built, about forty, I guessed, with bushy brown hair and penetrating dark eyes.

"I'm John," said the other, who was thin, clean shaven, with green eyes. He looked to be younger, maybe in his late twenties. "Peace be upon you."

Mary Magdalene, Thomas, John? I thought to myself. Could it be?

With the food, drink and care, I recovered my presence of mind, but still couldn't explain what was happening. I was somehow in the present and in the past, also. Couldn't explain, but couldn't resist, either — so, as before, I went with it.

"What was that you were singing?" I asked.

"That," Thomas said, "is a hymn we used to sing to celebrate our Savior and Lord when we were with him."

Smith Peak

"And after..." said John, his voice trailing off.

"Yes," Thomas said, "Especially after."

There was a profound silence. They were dwelling in an enormous sadness. We sat in that silent sadness looking out at the long view— ridges, clouds, sky.

I visualized the violent death of Jesus.

Taken from his quiet camp by the soldiers of a brutal totalitarian regime, taunted in the streets by an angry mob, he was pegged onto a cross of rough timber by spikes through his hands and legs and left hanging in the desert heat to die. The Roman guard mocked him, posting a sign at the top of the cross that said, "King of the Jews." At the end, when he asked for a drink of water — *I thirst* — they offered him a sponge soaked in stinging vinegar. Can we imagine the pain, parched dry mouth, expecting a sponge soaked in sweet water instead?

This brutality and cruelty stood in vivid contrast to the elegant serenity of Sokrates' death I had witnessed the night before: a quiet interlude between trial and sentence, a thoughtful conversation on the journey of the soul, the elegant self-administered poison, and the slow, peaceful withdrawal from the body.

We put these teachers and philosophers on pedestals. We distance ourselves from them. They become historic artifacts, trapped in books. But when we see them as human beings, as

Yosemite Reverie

friends, we see the enormity of their sacrifice, how they give their wisdom to everyone, free of charge, without a thought for their own comfort, without caring how the world treats them, and we see how lost we are when they leave us.

In their leaving us they also give. They give us the ultimate lesson on how to surrender, how to die. And learning how to die, they say, is the only way to learn how to live.

Mary finished bandaging my arm and feet and leaned back, her hands folded on her lap.

"Thank you, thank you" I said, as I felt the tight wrap soothe my arm, "May I ask a question?"

They nodded.

"What was he like? I mean, who was he?"

"Not who was he," John said, "but who is he.

"Not was — *is*," he repeated.

"Who *is* he?" I asked, not understanding, since he had lived more than two thousand years ago.

"I remember when we were confronted by the mob in the Tabernacle," John answered, a sad smile on his face. I noticed a light in his eyes also.

"He had made a big stir by then. He was shaking up their beliefs and traditions. We were surrounded by an angry mob. Our Lord said to them, *You are from beneath; I am from above: you are of this world; I am not of this world.*

"Naturally, they didn't like this, and they didn't understand who would have the audacity to make these claims, so they said to him, 'Who are you?'"

"I've wondered that very thing myself when talking with my master," I volunteered. "He can be so confounding, so challenging. I mean, if I'm honest, I have to admit, I also sometimes wonder to myself, who are you?"

"That's right," John said, "That's why I always say: *the light shines in the darkness, and the darkness can't grasp it.* Our minds are darkness, and we can't get hold of the idea that the Word can be made flesh, that someone can be both man and God at the same time — even when he's standing in front of us!"

"Yes, very hard to comprehend."

"Anyway, there in the Tabernacle, when they asked him, 'Who are you?' he said to them, *When you've lifted up the Son of man, then you'll know that I am he, and that I do nothing of myself; but as my Father has taught me, I speak these things.*"

"I think I get it," I said. "He's saying masters live in the Divine Will. They've surrendered, they're One with the One. They don't do anything on their own. We only realize it when we realize the master within, when we've raised our consciousness to his level, when we've 'lifted up the Son of man.'"

"Yes," John said, "that's right.

Yosemite Reverie

"Then he turned from the mob and said to our little group, "If you continue in my *Logos* — in my Word — then you are my disciples indeed; And you shall know the truth, and the truth shall make you free.

"He's telling us," John went on, "that if we keep practicing the *Logos*, if we keep meditating, keep knocking at the door, we'll be real disciples, we'll know the truth and be free. Imagine what he's offering: real truth, real freedom."

"It reminds me of the Hindu saying, that spirituality is *sat-chit-ananda* — truth, consciousness, bliss."

"Yes."

"What did the mob say? How did they respond to this offer?"

"With pride," John said sadly, "Anger.

"They challenged him: 'We're descendants of Abraham — the old prophet, and we've never been in bondage to anyone: how can you dare say you'll make us free?'

"They thought, 'We're not slaves. We're proud of our heritage. We escaped bondage in Egypt. We're already free. How can you say you'll free us?'

"See, this is our problem," John added, "We think we're free, but we're really slaves... slaves to our desires, slaves to our bodies, slaves to our to culture, social standing. The mind can't grasp this simple truth: that until we've gone beyond all this we're slaves.

"And then they just couldn't take it from this young rabbi

with a black beard. In our culture, so bound by tradition, if you don't have a white beard you're nobody, you're zero.

"'You're not even fifty years old,' they yelled. As if age has anything to do with spirituality!" John said pumping his fist in the air as he talked.

"Then they challenged him again: 'Have you even seen Abraham?' So much pride and attachment to the old ways, the old teachers. I mean, the prophets were great, but here in front of them was a living master!

"'What do you know,' they're saying, 'You haven't even seen Abraham.' They reduced everything to the physical.

"So Jesus said to them, *I'm telling you the truth: Before Abraham was, I am.*

"*I am,*" John repeated, "'I was,' would make grammatical sense, since Abraham lived a long time before, and he's saying he was there before even then. But he said, '*I am.*'

"He's pointing to the universal nature of the Word Made Flesh — the master. He's timeless, not time bound. He exists outside of time and for all time, both at once."

"You mean not in the future, not in the past," I said, "but in the Eternal Now."

"Yes," John continued, "He's offering freedom, truth. And how did they respond? With stones. He had to hide himself and sneak out. Otherwise they would've killed him right then and there."

Yosemite Reverie

Thomas looked up from the ground and said, "Whenever we would talk with him about the Prophets like Abraham and Moses, he used to admonish us: *You have dismissed the Living One who is before you and you have spoken about the dead.* Even we didn't appreciate what we had when he was with us."

"That's what my own master used to say, also," I added, "*We persecute the living and we worship the dead.*"

"Yes, sadly," John said. "And in a strange way, that's why he had to leave. He told us, 'It's good for you that I go away: for if I don't go away, the Comforter won't come to you; but if I depart, I will send it to you.

"That was the hardest thing of all. He meant we were too attached to him physically. It was so wonderful just to be with him, to share bread, to hear his sermons. But he knew even that attachment can hold us back. He knew that when we could no longer find him outside, we'd have to look inside... for the Comforter, the Holy Ghost."

"That's when we really began to appreciate him," Thomas said. "After he left. That was his plan."

"I get the plan," John replied, "I just never liked it."

"Remember, John, how he used to tell us the most important thing was to seek within?

"Yes, he often said, *If you bring forth what is within you,* what you bring forth will save you. But if you do not bring forth what is within you, what you do not bring forth will destroy you."

"Yes, I remember."

"You see," Thomas went on, "it all boils down to having our own experience. We need the Living Christ to get us started. We need that attachment. We need the Word Made Flesh to start us on the path. But ultimately, he taught us, we need our own experience, we have to find the True Christ, the True Light within.

"Jesus used to challenge us," Thomas said, "*If they say to you, 'Where did you come from?', say to them, 'We came from the light, the place where the light came into being by itself....' If they say to you, 'Who are you?' say, 'We are its children, we are the elect of the living father.' If they ask you, 'What is the sign of your father in you?', say to them, 'It is movement and repose.'*

I thought one of the oldest instruction on meditation, from the Yoga Sutras of Patanjali: *yoga chitta vritti nirodha*, 'meditation is a stilling of the waves of the mind.'

"*Movement and repose*," Thomas repeated, "That's the inner practice. Bringing the waves of the mind to stillness and seeing the light within. He always emphasized looking within, knowing ourselves."

"It's the same as Sokrates!" I blurted out. It had been only

Yosemite Reverie

a few hours, but with the bear, and the Apostles and all, I had forgotten about last night's dialogue until now, "Sokrates always said: 'Know thyself!'"

"Right," Thomas said, nodding. "As Jesus told us, *if you do not know yourselves, then you are in poverty and you are poverty.*"

"These are such beautiful sayings of Jesus," I said, "it's a shame none of them made it into the Bible."

"Bible?" Thomas asked.

"Yes," I said, "None of these things Jesus said to you are in the Bible. John has a chapter, but you don't."

"What's the Bible?" John asked.

"You don't know?"

"Know what?"

"Don't you know anything about what's happened in the last two thousand years?"

"Two thousand years?"

"What are you talking about?"

"Well, Christianity is the world's largest religion."

"Christianity?" Thomas asked, "What does that mean?"

"The religion of Christ, the people who worship Jesus Christ are called Christians."

John, Mary, and Thomas looked at each other, perplexed.

"I don't understand," John said. "After he left us, we went off in different directions. We told anyone who would listen about him, about his teaching. And each of us wrote down whatever we could remember, or the people around us wrote down what they heard us say, and we would share notes and sing together and remember him."

"It wasn't easy," Thomas added. "We were hunted by the Romans — they thought we threatened their pagan gods. And some of the Jews objected to us, too. That was the strangest thing, because we ourselves were Jews. Some thought we were misinterpreting the Prophets. But we just wanted to be left alone to remember our beloved rabbi and seek the Comforter within.

"He didn't want to start a new religion. All he ever did was try to help us understand the true meaning of our own religion, to free us from concepts and get to the core."

"Yes, yes, I understand," I answered, "But later, maybe a hundred or two hundred years later, it started to form as a separate religion, called Christianity.

"People started to believe, drawn by the message of love and transcendence, and, to be honest, by his dramatic death. But they were persecuted and isolated. There were many groups and subgroups, spread all over the Mediterranean basin, and beyond, captivated by his spirit and his story."

"I know," Thomas said, "I ended up in India."

"And I settled in Ephesus, and taught there," said John.

Ephesus? I thought, *that's where Herakleitos lived!*

Yosemite Reverie

Herakleitos emphasized *Logos* more than any other Greek philosopher. And John emphasized *Logos* more than any other Apostle. I wondered if John settled in Ephesus because Herakleitos had started a *Logos* school there only a few centuries earlier. John certainly would have known about it . . . .

"Anyway," I went on, returning to myself, "each group developed its own style, its own interpretations, own writings, own leaders and hierarchies. You can imagine — it became political. Groups argued about who was right, who was closest to Jesus, and so on, as people do.

"One well known writer, Irenaeus — they call him a 'Church Father' — he decided that some of the writings were good and some were bad. He called the bad ones 'heresies.'

"Irenaeus?" John asked. "Never heard of him."

"He lived a couple of hundred years after, and he said your book," I said, turning to Thomas, "was heresy. So it was banned."

"Thomas' book 'heresy'?" John asked, incredulous. "How can someone say that. My brother here only wrote down the beautiful sayings of our Lord. How can that be heresy?"

"Well, Irenaeus didn't like it," I said, "so when the Roman Emperor, Constantine — another hundred years after Irenaeus — decided to become a Christian, he made Christianity the official religion of the Roman Empire...."

"Wait, what?!" John asked, "First someone who never met

him decides what he really said, then the Empire who killed him — and hunted us — makes a religion in his name and claims him? This is too much."

"Yes, it's true. I'm sorry," I said, "Should I stop?"

"No, go on," they said. Mary, all this time remained quiet, serene, hands folded in her lap, looking at the ground.

"OK. So, Constantine the Emperor ordered all the Church leaders to come to a big convention — now this is about a hundred years after Irenaeus and about three hundred years after Jesus. They voted on which writings and doctrines were true and which were false...."

"Voted?" John interrupted. "How can you vote on Truth?"

"Well, they did. And they decided the winners were the only true and correct teachings — they called them orthodox — and banished the uh, losers.... Sorry Thomas," I said.

I paused, but he didn't answer.

"Anyway," I went on, "they got rid of the 'heretics,' if you'll excuse the expression. Their writings, their position, their standing. They were all out.

"Then they organized the ones who were in, the orthodox, into one big church. It became the official doctrine, the correct teachings of Jesus, with the Emperor's power behind it. They called it the *catholic* church."

"That's ironic," John said, "catholic means 'universal,' or

'whole.' And their idea of 'wholeness' was to throw half the people out."

"Maybe so," I said, "but Constantine's 'orthodox' writings became the official canon of the Catholic Church, the Bible we have today."

"Bible? It just means 'book.'" Thomas said.

"Yes. But not just a book," I answered, "*The Book*, The Bible.

"It was a revolutionary technology: written words bound together. It was compact, transportable, and you could make copies. Much better than the old scrolls. They collected all the orthodox writings, and put them in one book. It was very effective at spreading the message — and standardizing it, too.

"And today it's the most widely published book in the world."

"Praise be!" Thomas said.

"But your stuff isn't in it," I said.

"Yeah, you mentioned that."

"No hard feelings?" I asked. He just smiled at me. I could see he was lost in his thoughts, trying to process all this information.

"They said your stuff was heresy," I said to him, "It was banned. And anybody caught with heresy was condemned to hell. People believed deeply in the power of the Church. Eternal damnation horrified them — naturally. And some of the heretics were beheaded, tortured — to make examples out of them."

"Still more killing," Thomas said, a tear running down his cheek.

"So almost all the 'heresies' were destroyed," I continued. "Actually, until about seventy-five years ago your gospel had been lost. All we knew of it were a few parts that Irenaeus and other critics quoted when they were refuting it.

"Then, in 1945 a copy of it was found in an earthen jar buried in the mountains near Cairo. Apparently some early Christians far from the center of power didn't go along with the Emperor. Guess they're the ones who lost the vote.

"So instead of destroying the so-called heresies, they buried them deep in a cave — your book, the Gospel of Truth, Gospel of Philip, and others. They were all found in a cave in 1945. Took another few decades for scholars to translate and publish them.

"Now your book," I continued talking to Thomas, "Is the most popular of the newly discovered texts. But it's still not part of the Bible, it's not considered correct — orthodox — not officially. One well-respected modern Bible scholar called it 'rubbish.'"

"My Lord," John said, shaking his head. "It's nothing but our rabbi's sayings collected by Thomas himself."

"And with the discipline of the Catholic Church, the technology of the Book, and the power of the Emperor behind them, the Christians went on to conquer most of the world. They

Yosemite Reverie

formed nations and armies, fought wars and claimed land, all in Jesus' name. They even went to distant places, and forced the people there to give up their ways of worshiping the Creator and worship Jesus instead."

"Wait a second," Thomas said, coming back to the conversation, "you said my gospel was found in 'nineteen forty five.' What does that mean?"

"Oh," I said. "Sorry. As I mentioned, it's been two thousand years. Christianity is the most powerful religion in the world. Since the powerful make the rules, years now are numbered starting from the date of Jesus' birth. 'Nineteen forty five' means one thousand nine hundred forty five years since the birth of Christ, or, as the church calls it, *Anno Domini,* the year of our Lord.

"Wait," said Thomas, "You mean they don't count the Year of the Emperor?"

"Oh, there hasn't been a Roman Emperor for more than a thousand years," I said. "And every year in late December, the whole world celebrates the birth of Jesus in a holiday we call Christmas — or the Mass of Christ."

"But he was born in Spring," Mary said laughing, unable to contain herself. "Late December — that's the Roman winter solstice festival — it celebrates the return of the sun!"

"Yes," I said, "a Roman Emperor decreed December 25th to

be Jesus' birthday. He simply substituted the biggest Christian holiday for the biggest pagan holiday. Keeping the holiday more or less the same made it easier. People could adopt the new religion without giving up their favorite festival."

"How can anybody worship him without seeing him?" John asked, "without meeting him? That's not possible! He always said, *No man comes to the Father but by me*. He was always emphasizing the need for the master. He was so amazing. There's no way you could imagine it or understand it without being with him."

"Yes," I said, "But the Church says that Jesus is master for everyone, for all time, there's no other. One of the lines from your gospel is quoted all around the world to prove it: For God so loved the world, that he gave his one and only Son, that whoever believes in him shall not perish, but have eternal life."

"What do you mean 'his one and only son?'" John said, "He always told us we could all become sons — and daughters," he said, glancing at Mary, "of God."

"Well it's been translated as 'his only son' for centuries," I said. "Most scholars admit there's not much justification for 'only son' in the text. It really means something like the uniquely qualified one, emphasizing the uniqueness of the master."

"Yes, yes," said John. "I didn't mean 'the only son,' I meant 'only the son.' Only through the master can we realize the divine."

Yosemite Reverie

"That's the problem with words," I said. "They can be misinterpreted, mistranslated."

"But it makes no sense," John said. "How can you be saved by someone you've never met? How does that work? Our master always said, *I must work the works of him that sent me, while it is day: the night cometh, when no man can work.*

"He could only work during his lifetime — day is life, night is death," John explained, "He came only for his allotted sheep, for those of us who knew him while he was alive. That's why the Word comes into the flesh — to be with us person-to-person.

"I mean," John went on, "If we could worship a past rabbi, then we didn't need the Word Made Flesh. We could have worshiped Moses, or Abraham.

"What was the whole point of Jesus coming — and suffering? He came like all living masters come, to shake us out of our concepts, our beliefs. As he told them, ye worship ye know not what!"

"We needed his living example of love, of surrender to His Father's will, to understand."

"Yes, yes," I said, "My master, Maharaji, always said past masters, no matter how great they were, are as far away from us as the Father himself, so we might as well worship the Father directly — but we can't, because we can't relate to a concept.

"He often talked about your master, about how beautiful his teachings were. But he pointed out that the Bible didn't contain his exact words, it was written much later — you can't read it as a book of law.

"And he also pointed out that everybody who says they worship Christ has a different concept. In Northern Europe, they paint him with fair skin, blond hair and blue eyes. In Southern Europe: dark skin, black hair and brown eyes. They paint what they like, and they put it up and worship it.

"'We can only love what we can see,' Maharaji always said, 'that's why we require this medium of the living master. Because we can love them, we can know them, we can see them.'"

"Yes," John said, "The Word was made flesh and dwelt among us."

"But it's really amazing when you think about it," I went on, "there's so much devotion in the world for Jesus — even still. Some people give up everything to serve him. They don't marry— they feel they are married to him. They don't work for money, they work in charity in his name. They live to serve him, and they try follow his example of love by serving humanity.

"There are so many good works being done in his name, so much devotion and love for him, even after centuries. And there are great masterpieces of art, music, architecture — all inspired by him. And even today, two thousand years later, there's a Pope in Rome..."

Yosemite Reverie

"A papa?" Mary asked.

"Yes, a Pope, a holy father. They say he's a direct descendant of Peter, the rock upon which Jesus built the Church. Because the Emperor was in Rome, and Christianity was the official religion, the head of the Church in Rome became the head of the entire Catholic Church, a spiritual emperor.

"Today the Catholic Church is spread across the whole world, and the Pope is loved by millions. He gets his inspiration from Jesus, and he has tremendous spiritual authority.

"So it's really quite amazing how, being two thousand years gone, the spirit of Jesus still inspires and animates so many people, so deeply."

3

There was another silence. They were absorbing the information. Guess even saints at their level, when in the body, have to process.

Then John turned to me and asked, "Why was Thomas' book banned, exactly?"

"That's a tough one," I said, taking a deep breath. "It boils down to this, I think. There're two aspects to spirituality: the outer and the inner. In India they call it *guru bhakti and nam bhakti*.

"Guru bhakti means devotion to the guru, love for the teacher, becoming attached to him. The guru is a person like us, but he's attached to the Word. The Word dwells in him, so our attachment to the guru, the "Christ" — unlike other attachments — leads us to the Divine.

"Nam bhakti means devotion to the Name within, or the Word, the *Logos*, the Holy Ghost or Comforter, as you would call it. This is the true form of the master. He's the Word made flesh — take away the flesh and you have only the Word.

Yosemite Reverie

"As Guru Nanak, one of the great saints of Northern India said, *shabd guru surat dhun chela*. It means 'The real form of the master is the Sound Current — they call it *shabd*, you call it *Logos* — and the real form of the disciple is the soul attuned to the Word within.

"It starts with devotion to the master — *guru bhakti*. But that's the means, not the end. The end, the purpose, the goal is devotion to the Word, to having our own experience — *nam bhakti*.

"Now Brother John, you emphasized devotion, or you could say *guru bhakti*. Your Gospel tells the compelling story of Jesus as a man. It starts with Jesus in the Temple, breaking the furniture, telling the money changers to get out, and challenging the religious practices that had grown up over the centuries."

"Make not my father's house a house of merchandise!" John repeated to himself with intensity, "Yes, I remember that first visit to the Temple when he turned over the tables and chased out the money lenders. I mean, it's supposed to be a place of prayer, not commerce!"

"Yes. This was no meek rabbi," I said, "He was literally tearing up the place. He was challenging the authorities — very bold. But you also described his tender mercy — how he healed the sick, gave eyesight to the blind, forgave the woman caught in adultery, and so many other beautiful things he did."

"Yes," John agreed, his eyes welling, "I would give anything to be with my Beloved Lord again. There's no salvation without the master," John said authoritatively, "Only the son of God can do that. Without him, there's nothing. You have to believe in the master, and by believing in him you have life in his Name."

"True," I said, "and that's the key thing. You emphasized Jesus as the unique son of God, and the need to believe in and be devoted to the master.

"But Thomas here, he emphasized the inner quest, inner experience, devotion to the *Logos*, or you could say *nam bhakti*. Your book doesn't tell the story of the master's life, it doesn't tell any story at all. It only quotes his sayings, his teachings, meant to spur us on to our own experience.

"John emphasized the master's life, his example, his story, how 'only the Son' can save us. Thomas emphasized the need for all of us to become sons of the Father, to have that inner experience for ourselves."

"Yes," Thomas said, " He used to tell us, *If those who lead you say to you, 'See, the kingdom is in the sky,' then the birds of the sky will precede you. If they say to you, 'It is in the sea,' then the fish will precede you. Rather, the kingdom is inside of you, and it is outside of you. When you come to know yourselves, then you will become known, and you will realize that it is you who are the sons of the living father.*

Yosemite Reverie

"Not only one son," Thomas repeated, "he said we all have the capacity to become sons of the living father,"

"And that was the main argument in the early Church," I said. "Some wanted to claim that Jesus was the only son of God, and all anybody had to do was believe in him to become Christian.

"Others said, no, he was one of the sons of God, one of a line of spiritual adepts, and anyone can realize the same divinity by following a master who teaches how to worship the Word within. It came down to a debate between those who said belief was enough and those who said you had to go beyond belief, you had to have your own experience, you had to know for yourself.

"Because Thomas and the other so-called 'heretics' emphasized self-knowing, the scholars call them Gnostics."

Now Thomas and John started laughing.

"What's so funny?" I asked.

"This is the thing we always used to bicker about," John said. "Thomas here was always going on and on about you can't have perfect faith without experience.

"I always said just believe in the master, the Christ, and he will take care of everything. It kind of became a running joke among all of us. 'Oh, there's goes Thomas, again, asking questions. Stop doubting, man, and believe!'"

"Well of course I had my doubts," Thomas quipped. "Nobody can have perfect faith without experience."

I began to see they were two old friends who had built their friendship around a perennial argument.

"Come on, have faith," John said, "He'll take care of everything."

"Faith without experience will always be shaky," Thomas countered. "I mean if someone says 'This is the sweetest dessert,' you may believe him out of respect. But you won't absolutely know for sure that it's sweet without tasting it for yourself."

"You just need faith in the master," John said becoming wistful, "It's all about Him. I mean, if we had written it all down, the amazing things he did, even the whole world could not contain all the books that we'd have written."

"Amen, John. There's so much wonderful to say about him. But belief isn't enough. We can't stop there. We have to be doers of the Word."

The bickering continued, half in jest and half serious. Then Mary held up her hand. They immediately stopped, and looked down at the ground. I sensed they had an enormous respect — no, reverence — for her.

"You're both right," she said. "It's two sides of the same coin. I was closer to our Lord and Savior than any of you. He gave me his secret teaching — a teaching he gave to no-one else. You need both: the Word made flesh and your own experience of the Holy Ghost."

Yosemite Reverie

I remembered the *Gospel of Mary*, another of the so-called heresies. Only a fragment has survived, found in 1896. Mary is depicted as the foremost disciple of Jesus, closest to him. Even in the official catholic Bible she's the only one to witness all three: crucifixion, burial and resurrection. The *Gospel of Mary* said Jesus had given her 'secret teachings' that he hadn't given to any of the men. Some of the male apostles worshiped her, others were resentful.

The popular notion is that Mary Magdalene was a prostitute, a harlot. But there's no evidence in the Bible or any of the historic record for that: it was made up by Pope Gregory in 591. This fabrication was repeated so many times by people in authority that it gradually became accepted as fact.

It was more likely Mary Magdalene was Jesus' wife, his companion. And it made sense that the wife of a spiritual master could become the master when the husband passes to the other side.

There's a certain naturalness to it: the wife is closest to the Saint, understands him, and is known and respected by the community. Of course, if she's also a devoted disciple — seeing her husband not as a husband but as a spiritual teacher — she can become adept in her own right and give light.

"Our brother here has told us how our Lord's plan has unfolded over time. It's all his will," Mary said, "Our Lord had to go through all that to show what it means to surrender to the Will of the Father. Without that violent, horrible day, no one would have paid any attention to him, to his message. Now the whole world benefits from his example, and he inspires millions.

"It's his play, and we are only instruments. As he said so many times, I came down from heaven, not to do mine own will, but the will of him that sent me."

With these soothing words the whole atmosphere changed. Thomas and John were silent.

"Now you two each have your own approach. One emphasizes belief, and the other experience. Both are necessary."

"Sister," I said to her, looking into her two eyes, pools of love and understanding, "It reminds me of something beautiful my master wrote towards the end of his life: *May your love of the Form culminate in the love of the Formless.*"

"Precisely," she said.

Yosemite Reverie

4

I was so absorbed in conversation I hadn't noticed the weather change.

A heavy fog had rolled in. We could no longer see even the trees nearby.

Out of the fog came one of the other men. He bowed to Mary in reverence, leaned over, whispered something in her ear, and then walked back into the mist.

"Brother," she said to me, "It's time for us to go. Would you like to see us off?"

"Yes."

She rose — serene, elegant, graceful. John, Thomas and I followed.

As we walked in the mist, following close behind so as not to lose her, I heard singing in the near distance. It was the *Logos* hymn again. We followed her around a large tree. The entire group was standing in front of us, singing, carrying bundles made of thick blankets.

"Brother, here, these are yours," she said, handing me my

cotton sweats, dry and neatly folded. They must have collected them when they found me under the rock. As they prepared their bundles, I went behind a tree and changed back into my own clothes. When I came out and returned the robe and blanket to Mary, John gave me a small satchel with bread and a flask of drink, "you'll need this."

Thomas took off his sandals and held them out, "You'll need these, too, brother."

"So grateful to you . . . to you all," I said.

"No, we are grateful to you," John said, "We now see how our Lord's plan turned out, why he had to suffer, why we were persecuted and had to spread out. It spread his message of love and truth. And it still touches so many and for such a long time."

"Peace be upon you, my son" Mary said, holding her hand over my head in blessing. I felt a wave of love and elation.

She turned and walked towards the singing. The entire group was moving away, voices weaving in and out in ethereal harmony. It was hard to tell in the mist, but it looked like they were walking upwards, one by one, into the cloud, as if on a staircase.

I walked towards them as fast as I could. I wanted to follow. I wanted to rise. But something stopped me. I could go no further.

I could only stand on that mountain top, earthbound, and listen to the voices recede into the mist:

Yosemite Reverie

Ἐν ἀρχῇ ἦν ὁ λόγος,
καὶ ὁ λόγος ἦν πρὸς τὸν θεόν,
καὶ θεὸς ἦν ὁ λόγος . . . .

In the beginning was the *Logos*,
and the *Logos* was with God,
and the *Logos* was God . . . .

VI. Return

Yosemite Reverie

1

As the voices faded the sun came out, the mist burned off and I was alone in a clear blue day. I walked around the mountain-top camp. They were gone. Where'd they go?

I began to feel cold and started walking. Thomas' sandals were surprisingly comfortable, and my feet were much better. Something special in Mary's poultice.

Wasn't far to the intersection of the trails, so I decided to go back to Ten Lakes. Maybe the bears were gone. I could get my stuff. Would love to put on the down parka and boots. Anyway, I needed the car key — zipped in the pack — to get home.

After about an hour's walk my abandoned campsite appeared. I crept carefully, looking around. In the clearing was the rock where Sokrates gave his last satsang. Nearby my pack, sleeping bag, and other gear spilling out on the ground. No sign of the bears.

I clapped my hands to flush them out. Nothing.

Feeling more confident I walked in. I was alone. The bears had carefully unzipped every pocket of the backpack, ripped opened every food pouch and eaten all the food. Nothing was damaged.

Return

It was getting late, and windy. Another storm? Body was tired from all the action, and mind was blown.

Needed sleep.

So I set up the tent, blew up the thermarest, and fluffed up the sleeping bag inside. Then I collected the gear from all over the place and repacked it. I munched on some of John's bread, strung the rest high in a tree, returned to the tent, kicked Thomas' sandals off outside, slithered in and zipped the door.

Cozy in that little nylon world, safe from the wind and damp outside, I rolled the down jacket into a makeshift pillow and tucked it under my head, the *Logos* hymn repeating in my mind, and drifted to sleep.

Yosemite Reverie

2

I slept a very long time. Was awakened by songbirds greeting the dawn, and sat in the tent determined to still my mind. I started to meditate — Repetition, Contemplation, Listening — but my thoughts kept racing, going over the improbable encounters of the past days — Herakleitos' zen aphorisms on the first night, Sokrates' heart-rending last day, the attack by a reluctant bear, being lost in a storm, being found by Mary, John and Thomas, the conversation about Jesus — and the ethereal *Logos* hymn.

After a little while I couldn't stand the racing mind and the sun's heat beating through the nylon tent. I crawled out, stood up, stretched, felt my arm, and noticed the scab encrusted gash.

I fired up the stove and put water on to boil. Bears had eaten the sugar and powdered milk but hadn't touched the tea. Brought the bundle down and finished John's loaf with plain tea.

I was sore, tired and out of food. It was time to go. Laced up my boots — trusty boots. Little painful on the sore feet but felt

Return

good to put them on. Stowed the sandals in the outside pouch. Stuffed the bag, rolled the pad, struck the tent.

I hoisted the pack on my back, cinched the breast strap and the belt. It was pretty light now with no food. I picked up the remaining walking stick and took a moment to look around — camp was clean. No trace of what happened here. Didn't make sense, anyway. But happen it did.

I wheeled around and strode out. After a few minutes I found my rhythm again — breath, stick, stride — and sailed down the trail, retracing my steps along the Tuolumne, this time following it gently upstream.

When I got to Glen Aulin campground, where I had met Herakleitos three nights earlier at the river, I swung away from the river, crested the ridge, and began to retrace my steps down the trail towards the Visitor Center where I'd left the car.

After only a few minutes heading down, I heard footsteps crashing behind, and without looking back, stepped aside. A man brushed by in a hurry.

He was thin, with a high forehead, a shock of gray hair, and a closely cropped white beard. He wore rough loose clothing and leather sandals, awkwardly stumbling down the trail, mumbling something to himself in a strange language.

Yosemite Reverie

Again? I thought. *Who's it this time?*

He stopped a few paces ahead and tacked a piece of parchment to the trunk of a tall fir, using the fat top end of his walking stick as a hammer and a stout sharp broken twig as a nail.

"Wait, wait, master!" a voice from behind called. Another man rushed past. He was also bearded, wearing rough robes, but younger, and agile. He clutched scraps of parchment and was out of breath from running. "Sir! Please," he shouted, "Wait!"

The first man stopped pounding on the tree and looked back.

"Porphyry, my boy, keep up," he said, impatiently.

"Yes, sir, sorry, sir," the second man said, stopping at the tree, panting. "I just can't collect all these pages as fast as you're writing them."

"Well I can't wait for you to catch up."

"Yes sir."

Then the first man turned to me and, coming up close, leaned into my face and asked, "Who are you?"

"Um, I'm, uh..."

"Doesn't matter," he said. "Let's sit. Maybe Porphyry here can make some use of himself while he catches his breath.

"Pour us a drink."

"Yes, Plotinus, sir," Porphyry said, reaching into a sack and pulling out a fired clay flask.

"You can join us, too, if you want," he said to me, patting the

Return

rock next to him. I sat down. Porphyry handed me the flask and gestured for me to drink.

Plotinus lived in Rome about two hundred years after Jesus. Modern scholars call him a "Neo-Platonist," because he went back to basics — the philosophy of Sokrates and Plato. But in his own time he simply considered himself a philosopher, a seeker.

Living in Rome, he became the center of an influential circle of intellectuals. He was in the thick of the philosophical debates that raged around the formation of the Catholic Church. Now I seemed to be in the thick of a conversation with him myself.

"Here, Porphyry, how about this one?" Plotinus said, taking a parchment from a fold in his robe, and holding it out.

After Plotinus died in 269 AD, his foremost disciple, Porphyry, collected his writings — which Plotinus never organized or edited — and made them into a series of books. I was witnessing master and disciple in action.

Porphyry took the sheet from his master's outstretched arm and read it aloud:

Fire, air, water and earth are in themselves soulless, and there are no other elements in the body than these four....

Since none of these are alive, it would be extraordinary if life came about by simply mixing them together. It's impossible, in fact, that simply mashing up material elements should produce life . . . .

Yosemite Reverie

Porphyry paused. He seemed to be having a hard time making out the words. I needed the pause anyway, to absorb what Plotinus had written, which I took to mean that life didn't happen by itself.

Then Porphyry continued,

Furthermore, no one would pretend that results like the human body could happen by a chance mixing of these things — some guiding principle must be necessary, some Cause must direct the mixture. That guiding principle would be Soul.

The body — not merely because it's complex, but even if it were simple — could not exist unless there were Soul in everything. So body owes its existence because Logos *enters into matter, and only from Soul can* Logos *come.*

There it was again: *Logos*. Just as Herakleitos had said, and Sokrates, and the Apostles, Plotinus was saying that Logos is the creative power organizing and animating everything.

"Very nice, sir," Porphyry said looking up at his master, "very, very nice."

Then turning to me, he added, "When Plotinus here has written anything he can never bear to go over it twice. Even to read it through once is too much for him. His eyesight is bad. His handwriting is terrible, too. He doesn't divide his syllables correctly, and he pays no attention to spelling.

Return

"I wish he would take time to go back over these, because they're amazing. But I can't get him to do it. He's on fire, and this stuff pours out of him. Honestly, I myself can't understand him half the time."

"I see," I said.

"Here's another one," Plotinus said, reaching into another fold, handing another scrap to Porphyry. "This came to me last night."

Porphyry read:

Logos *is the ruler, making all. It wills things as they are, and according to* Logos *it produces even what we know as evil. It can't will everything to be good.*

An artist wouldn't make an animal all eyes, and in the same way, Logos *doesn't make everything divine.*

It makes gods and also celestial spirits, the intermediate order, then men, then the animals. Everything's on a continuum, and this isn't in a spirit of malice, but it's the expression of a Logos *that is teeming with variety.*

Now, we're like people who don't know anything about painting who complain that the colors aren't beautiful everywhere in the picture. But the Artist has put the appropriate color on every spot.

Or we're criticizing a play because the characters are not all heroes — but there's a servant, and a country

Yosemite Reverie

bumpkin, and some humble clown. Yet take away the low characters and the power of the drama is gone. They're all part and parcel of it.

"Yes, my master always said we're simply actors in a play," I said without thinking, "Someone is a villain, someone a hero, but at the end of the play, there's no reality to it."

"And this," Plotinus said, paying no attention to me, handing another parchment to Porphyry.

If this universe is the direct creation of Logos *applying itself, completely unchanged, to Matter... then its product must be excellent and perfect. . . .*

But, it will be asked, hasn't it, besides itself entering into matter, brought other beings down? Has it not, for example, brought souls into matter, and, in adapting them to its creation, twisted them against their own nature and ruined many of them? And can this be right?

The answer is that souls are, in a fair sense, part of Logos.

And Logos *has not adapted souls to the creation by perverting them, but has set them in the place here to which their quality entitles them.*

"Wait," I blurted out, "you're going too fast."

Return

Porphyry stopped reading and they both looked at me.

"Are you saying," I asked, "that *Logos* creates every soul into a form, or a body, that suits them based on their inherent qualities? It sounds like karma theory — we get what we deserve, we follow our desires."

"Keep reading," Plotinus said to Porphyry, then to me, "I've covered that, listen. . . ."

He was intense, but he was charming, also, and I found myself being drawn in.

Porphyry looked down again, took a moment to find his place on the scrawling sheet, and went on:

And we shouldn't minimize the obvious — that we have to think about more than the present. There's the past and the future; and these have everything to do with fixing the value of place.

So a man, once a ruler, will become a slave because he abused his power and because the fall is to his future good. Those that have misused wealth will be made poor — and poverty isn't a problem for people who are good.

Those that have unjustly killed are killed in turn — unjustly as regards the murderer but justly as regards the victim. And those that are to suffer are thrown into the path of those that give them the suffering they deserve.

Yosemite Reverie

It's not an accident that makes a man a slave. No one is a prisoner by chance. Every bodily outrage has its cause. The man once did what he now suffers. A man that murders his mother will become a woman and be murdered by her son. A man that wrongs a woman will become a woman, to be wronged.

Hence arises that awesome word, Adrasteia — *the Inescapable. For in truth this arrangement is Inescapable: absolute justice and an awesome wisdom.*

"Wow," I said. "It sure sounds like karma theory to me. You're just giving it a different name: The Inescapable.

"Didn't Sokrates say the same thing? Gluttonous people become donkeys, murderers become hawks — something like that?"

"Sokrates?" Plotinus asked, turning his gaze at me.

"Read him the bit about Sokrates," he said to his disciple.

"Um, yes, yes, sir," Porphyry said, rustling through a sack he had been carrying over his shoulder, "Let me find it.... here, here it is!"

Then he read:

It's like this: the visible Sokrates is a man, yet we make a painting of him and give the name of Sokrates to the image, which is just made up of colors, pigments.

In the same way, it's Logos *which makes up Sokrates,*

> *but we apply the name 'Sokrates' to the Sokrates we see. In reality, however, the colors and shapes which make up the Sokrates we see are just reproductions of the colors and shapes in the* Logos, *and this outer* Logos *has a similar relationship to the truest* Logos *of man.*

"And so much for that," Plotinus said when Porphyry had finished.

"That's why Sokrates told Crito 'Bury me any way you like, if you can find me!'" I said, getting excited, "You're also saying the real Sokrates is not the body. *Logos* is the real form. It gives shape to everything we see in the physical."

He turned to me with a penetrating, impatient stare.

"*Logos* is the beginning and *Logos* is everything and everything is made by It and arranged at birth entirely in this way," he said.

"I see, sir." He was very intense.

"Life and thought and all things come from the One," he went on, "and the One is not one of those things, but all things come from It — because It's formless. That One is One alone."

"It reminds me of Herakleitos!" I blurted out, "He said by listening to the *Logos*, we realize all things are One!"

Plotinus just sat silently. His eyes were on me but he seemed to be seeing within himself.

Yosemite Reverie

"What then is our way of escape, and how are we to find it?" he asked, to no-one in particular.

Then he answered his own question: "Our country from which we came is There. Our Father is There. How do we travel to it? Where's our way of escape?

"We cannot get There on foot — our feet only carry us around in this world, from one land to another. You mustn't ride a carriage, either, or a boat. Let all these things go — don't even look at them."

I instantly recalled the well-known lines from the Sikh gurus:
Seeing without eyes
Hearing without ears
Walking without feet...

"Shut your eyes," Plotinus went on, "change to — wake up to — another way of seeing — a way of seeing that everybody has available to them but few actually develop."

He was on a roll. Porphyry and I just kept quiet, listening. I closed my eyes and tried to imagine another way of seeing.

"And this inner vision, how does it work?" he asked.

I realized he had a habit of answering his own questions, so I waited.

"At first — when it's just awakened — the inner vision is too weak to bear the brilliance. The Soul must be trained to see all that beauty," he said, with authority.

Return

I thought again about the night of the starry sky when I was ten, and my inability to sustain that first breakthrough. Maybe my 'inner vision,' as Plotinus was saying, hadn't been developed — it was too weak, untrained.

So I asked him, "Trained, how?"

"Withdraw into yourself and look," he said, giving me a hard stare.

"Withdraw into yourself and look, and if you don't see beauty within yourself, then, just like someone who makes a beautiful statue cuts here and polishes there, and makes one part smooth and chisels another until he's made a beautiful face, so you also have to cut away excess and straighten the crooked and clear the dark and make it bright — and never stop working on your statue until the divine glory of virtue shines out of you, till you've achieved self-mastery!"

We start as a block of coarse stone, Plotinus was saying. Inside of that coarseness is something beautiful. We don't need to add anything. We only need to chip away the coarseness to reveal the hidden beauty that's already there.

I realized the chipping away of the stone block into a beautiful statue was a way to imagine the Repetition of the holy names that Maharaji had given me at initiation.

Repetition chips away the excess — one syllable at a time. To really do repetition with focused attention means to have no past, no future, no family, no friends, no worries, no hopes.

Yosemite Reverie

It chips away the excess — word after holy word — until nothing is left of the ego, the little self we call "I." When the little self is gone, all that's left is our true Self. Or to use Plotinus' image — when all of the excess is chiseled and polished, something truly beautiful is revealed — the True Self.

While I was lost in these thoughts, he started up again, rolling so fast and furious his words came out in bursts.

"If you've become this, and see it, and are at home with yourself in purity — with nothing stopping you from becoming One like this, with no inward mixture of anything else, but entirely yourself, nothing but True Light — immeasurable, boundless, limitless — everywhere unmeasured — because it's greater than all that can be measured and better than all that can be counted — when you see that you have become this — then you have become sight itself — you can trust yourself then, you have already ascended and need no one to show you — *concentrate your gaze and see!*"

He had really gotten himself worked up. Even though it was getting cold in that shaded canyon, he had broken into a light sweat. I found myself deeply attracted to his face.

We sat there together in silence, only the sound of wind through the tall pines and firs swaying above us. He seemed to have stopped for now, lost in his thoughts.

Return

Then he cleared his throat and said, "There's nothing random or by chance, no 'it just happened to be like this...' for he is the father of *Logos* — the cause and the things that are caused — all definitely far away from 'happening by chance.' He's free of coincidence. He is the cause of himself, for himself, and of himself. *He is simply what He is* — the original self and beyond the self.

"And this thing I'm talking about is lovable and love — love of himself — for he is beauty of himself and in himself — nothing else!"

Plotinus' words burst out in a pulsating torrent. He was unambiguous, unequivocal. He was insisting the light, the One, the divine — is right here, right in front of us, all we have to do is look and see.

But still I had a question.

"So how," I ventured, "how do we know we're on the right track?"

"Everything that exists has its existence by the One," he said, "The biggest puzzle is that understanding of the One is neither by reasoning nor by intellectual perception. It's rather a Presence better than knowledge.

"In what sense do we call it 'One'?," he went on, "The One isn't indivisible, as if it were the smallest thing. It's the greatest of all things — not in extent, but in power.

"And it must be understood as infinite not because its size

and number can't be measured or counted but because its power can't be comprehended."

"You mean it's like God, or mind?" I asked.

"When you think of it as God or as mind — it's more — it's more than you imagine it to be — for it exists in itself — without attributes."

"So when I wonder if I'm on the right track, you're saying there's no right or wrong — there's not even a track at all! Not even a place to reach, right?"

"It has no place. It doesn't need a place," he answered, "Other things come to a place because of the One. Because of it, they exist at the same time as they take up their assigned place. To seek a place is to be in need, and the Source is not in need of the things that come after it. The source of all things has no need for anything."

He gave me a long, deep, penetrating look. Yet I felt a deep kindness shining out. It was spell-binding.

"Don't form your vision by diverting your thought elsewhere. It doesn't lie somewhere — it's always present to anyone who's able to touch it."

"Always present," I repeated, "but how do we develop that vision, how do we touch it, reach it?"

Gesturing at the parchment he had tacked to the tree next to

Return

us, the one he had just put up before we started talking, he said to Porphyry, "read it to him."

Porphyry walked up to the tree, stepped on a rock at its base, stood on his tiptoes, pulled out the wood nail from the trunk with a grunt, took the sheet down and flattened it on his thigh.

It took him almost a full minute to read through. I could see him mumbling to himself trying to decipher the scrawl. Then, when he had it all worked out, he read:

We may know we have had the vision when the Soul has suddenly taken light. This light is from the Supreme and it is the Supreme....

Thus the Soul unlit remains without that vision. Lit, it possesses what it sought. And this is the true end set before the Soul, to take that light, to see the Supreme by the Supreme and not by the light of any other thing— to see the end which is also the means to the vision—

For the thing that illuminates the Soul is also the thing that sees, just as it is by the sun's own light that we see the sun.

And how is this to be accomplished?

Cut away everything.

"OK?" Plotinus asked when Porphyry had finished, looking straight at me with piercing eyes. "Got it? You want wisdom? Vision?

Yosemite Reverie

"*Cut away everything*," he said conclusively.

Then, to his disciple: "Let's go."

Plotinus stood up, grabbed his stick, and went scampering down the trail, with Porphyry trundling behind.

Return

3

I watched them disappear down the trail. Just as they approached a bend Plotinus darted off to the side and went crashing through the brush with his disciple dashing off behind him.

They were gone.

I can't say I was getting used to these encounters, but there seemed to be a pattern. On the first night I had met Herakleitos, one of the earliest known Greek philosophers, then Sokrates, who lived about a hundred years later, then the Apostles, who were about four hundred years after that. Now, it seemed, I had been face-to-face with Plotinus, and his disciple Porphyry, who lived two centuries after Christ.

Somehow, in the high Sierra, I was getting eight hundred years of Western philosophy in a few nights.

But I realized now that, to them, there was no "western" philosophy or "eastern." There was just philosophy, just the teachings, the Truth as they had discovered it for themselves, or learned it from their own masters. And it was the same, naturally, as I was learning from mine.

Yosemite Reverie

I realized, also, that in their time, the world wasn't divided into "east" and "west," as it is today. They all lived around a body of water they called the Sea in the Middle of the Land — because it was the center of their world. They would sail across it, or walk around it on foot or donkey, and come into contact with different philosophers or teachers, but they all shared a common culture.

It was only later, centuries later, that the cultures around the Mediterranean grew apart and developed discrete ways of looking at and thinking about what's common to all. Then, as they were driven further apart by religious wars and priestly classes interested in sowing division, these cultures began to claim sole ownership of the truth, accusing others of blasphemy or heresy and we divided ourselves into "East" and "West." The world is a globe, one small blue planet, and all these boundaries and divisions are created by us.

Cultures may have different flavors, or different styles, but the message of the philosophers and teachers and mystics is always the same. They're all pointing at the same thing — a creative power that leads to an inner knowing of the unity of all things. Over time, we focus on the pointing finger and forget what they're pointing at.

Herakleitos started by saying, *Listening not to me, but to the Logos, it's wise to agree that all things are One.*

Return

Sokrates demonstrated how to withdraw the attention from the physical world and focus on the metaphysical, with its promise of the True Earth for those who practiced philosophy correctly.

And the Apostles, invoking the words of their master Jesus, remind us how practice of the *Logos* — the Word — leads to truth and freedom.

Now, here, as I was making my return, Plotinus was saying the same thing: by cutting away the Many we realize the One — the *Logos* — the eternal presence that's right here, if only we would reach out and touch it.

I had come to the mountains with a question and a quest. My question was when I die, will I be dead forever? or is there something after? I had heard reassurance that, yes, the soul survives, and the well ordered soul finds happiness There.

And I had come on a quest: to still my mind. I had planned on seven nights of trekking deep in the high Sierra. I figured if I really tried, that'd be enough time.

I'd been gone three nights, and walked in a small disorganized circle. I'd carelessly exposed myself to hungry bears, gotten injured and lost, and was now without food and dead tired. Nothing had gone as planned, and I sure hadn't stilled my mind. What a fool I'd been.

Yosemite Reverie

But if I hadn't stilled my mind, maybe I could begin to enjoy my meditation. Maybe I could let go of goals, and progress, and expectation. Maybe simply be present and open myself.

I had a new perspective, a vivid clarity. I had experienced the company of these inspiring teachers — no longer abstract and bound to the page, or interpreted by scholars — but up close and personal. They confirmed the path Maharaji had shown me. They amplified my relationship with him.

They showed that life was not a fruitless exercise, just another turn on the wheel, but a precious opportunity. They gave reassurance that there was something after death, that the soul doesn't just fly off into nothing, but, if life is lived well, it can end in light, love, and lift.

They showed, above everything, the power of love — most essentially the love between master and disciple. I saw how Sokrates' students loved him, and how he loved them, how he died to show them what it means to be committed to Truth. I saw how the Apostles still lived in the presence of their beloved Christ, and how his bloody death was the ultimate example of surrender to the Father's will. I saw Porphyry literally following in his master's footsteps, wherever he would go, turning sharply left or right without hesitation, even into the thick forest — a true disciple. I realized what a gift I had in my association with

Maharaji, his loving guidance, and the continuing guidance and comfort being given by his successor in the decades since his departure.

"If you want to reach the abode of the Lord," Maharaji said, "you need only love and devotion. If you ask the name of the Lord, it is love, love, and love. If you ask whether the Lord belongs to a particular place or country, that also is only love. Love, and love alone, is the real form of the Lord."

It's foolish to set arbitrary deadlines, to have an expectation. Love can't be forced. Nature can't be forced. Spiritual evolution, awakening, is a natural process. All these teachers were saying: "you cannot hustle the Power within."

The seed is already there, I realized. I only need to cultivate it — to protect it, to water it, to expose it to light. Those were the positive steps I could take. But the seed grows by itself. It's natural. Automatically the consciousness comes into harmonic vibration with *Logos*.

As the Apostles sang in the *Logos* hymn, *Logos* does the work. All things were created by *It*. It was the Power within, *It* was the true form of the master. The master, the *Logos*, was arranging everything so that this soul could make its return to the One.

We think we're doing it, but actually, It's working through us. The philosopher Alan Watts often asked, with a twinkle in his eye, "Do *you* do it, or does *It* do you?"

Yosemite Reverie

But I also learned it wasn't going to happen in these mountains, and not overnight, or in a few nights. It was foolish to think I could force something to happen — in a week! The breakthrough, the rising, the unfolding, happens over time, it happens in the thick of things — it's a slow blossoming. I felt more confident now, more at peace. I was complete, content. All I needed to do was go home and tend to the garden of my life.

Slowly I rose from the rock, shouldered the pack, adjusted the straps, picked up the stick, put one foot in front of the other and followed the trail down to the car.

Return

4

One of the secrets of mountaineering is that the return can be more dangerous than the ascent. The ascent takes will — you have to muscle your way up.

But the return takes care — you have to prevent gravity from throwing you down. Now your muscles, instead of propelling you upwards against gravity, have to hold you back from gravity's relentless downward pull. That's the crux of staying alive, anyway — staying vertical — and in the end, gravity always lays us down.

With a heavy pack pushing from behind, you have to prevent a runaway descent and avoid a devastating ankle twist. It's all the more difficult because the descent is when fatigue and exhaustion can overtake you.

So I tried to put the encounters of the last few days out of my mind and focus only on the step in front of me. Step by step I strode along the path, breathing in and breathing out. I was at peace, calm, centered. One foot in front of the other and soon I was again at the place where the trail turns and the vista to the

Yosemite Reverie

trail-head opened up. I saw the Visitor Center in the distance, cars clustered around it, ships at port.

I stopped, leaned on my stick, and took one more drink of water. Then I stowed the flask and started the final push.

In no time at the car. I touched the rubber handle on the rear hatch, and because the electronic key fob was in the pack, the hatch opened automatically like an enormous jaw.

I unclipped the waist and breast straps, turned around, and dropped the pack on the rear deck, wiggling my arms free. Then I sat down, took off my boots and socks and looked at my feet. Not too bad. A little swollen, bruised, but no bleeding. I slipped on the sneakers I had left behind. They felt featherlight after days of heavy boots. Touched the button — the hatch closed itself.

I walked to the driver's side and opened the door.

The car erupted —

FLASH FLASH FLASH FLASH FLASH FLASH FLASH FLASH
HONK HONK HONK HONK HONK HONK HONK HONK

Somehow the thing had become unlocked without disarming. I ran back to the hatch, pressed the rubber handle, waited an eternity for the jaw to open again, dove for the pack, dragged it around and fumbled for the fob. In my exhaustion I couldn't remember where I'd stowed it, so I kept unzipping compartments, fishing around inside each of them, all the time —

Return

FLASH FLASH FLASH FLASH FLASH FLASH FLASH FLASH
HONK HONK HONK HONK HONK HONK HONK HONK

In the third pouch I found it, pulled it out, turned it around to find the unlock button and pressed it to finally silence the shrieking alarm.

The beast had become enraged. My nerves were shot.

I knelt hunched in the rear, took a deep breath, shoved the pack back in, closed the hatch again, put the fob in my pocket, walked to the driver's door, still open, and sat down.

I had been what seemed an eternity in silence and nature. I had epiphanies and transcendence. I had been at peace, centered, confident. Now, it was all shattered within moments of the first encounter with modern life.

I didn't want to engage with the machine, but I couldn't sit there forever. Anyway, I had already experienced the worst — that infernal car alarm and its endless shrieking. Now, at least, I can quietly drive home in the silence of my own company. I put my foot on the brake and pressed the START button.

The engine roared to life, the instrument panel lit up, and the satellite radio came on, blaring

"...MIGHT AS WELL FACE IT YOU'RE ADDICTED TO LOVE...."

The clear Sierra sky was shredded by drums, guitars, horns — rock 'n roll at a blasting volume.

Yosemite Reverie

I pressed the button to turn the radio off. But it wouldn't stop, *"...MIGHT AS WELL FACE IT YOU'RE ADDICTED TO LOVE..."*

I kept pressing the mute button as the instrument system was initializing but the radio would not stop. During startup there's no way to turn the damn thing off!

Finally, after about thirty seconds — an eon — the initialization completed, and the mute button worked.

Silence.

Now I was confronted with an array of glowing screens and digital information: a grainy map that degraded the majestic mountains to pixels of green traced by a grey line, a digital readout of temperature, time, elevation, miles traveled and so many other inconsequential ways of measuring.

I hammered the steering wheel with my fists and shrieked. I did not want to reenter. I did not want to lose the calm and clarity of these days.

Yet I couldn't stay here either. I needed to go home. I needed my wife, family, friends, home, my spiritual community, and those precious moments with my master. We don't belong to each other, he said, but we need each other. We support each other.

Is it possible to live in the world and still hold on to the mystery? I took a deep breath, put the car in gear, crept slowly downhill, and pointed back towards San Francisco Bay to find out.

Return

5

The car unwound itself around the mountains, descending, aiming at the sea. After about twenty minutes driving down Tioga Pass Road, I came to Olmsted Point, with a dramatic vista of Half Dome, Cloud's Rest, and the Yosemite Valley. I was still struggling with myself. The clarity I had felt only moments ago was becoming shrouded in the fog of thoughts and doubts again. So I pulled off.

The overlook was crowded with tourists — families, couples, a half-dozen languages. They stood by their cars in shorts and t-shirts near the interpretive signs, pointing at landmarks, taking selfies. Watching them I felt an overwhelming sense of oneness, compassion.

We were human, after all, and the differences of language, religion, nation, age, gender, social status, were trivial in comparison to the things we shared — the power within us, the need for love, and the fragility of life. I looked at each person and felt connected. We were all alive today, and some day we'd all face that terrifying transition we call 'death.'

Yosemite Reverie

I parked at the far end, got out and stood at the edge. I knew I had to re-enter, but still craved solitude. I realized what a profound gift I had been given, how here in the Yosemite I had seen that the philosophers and saints are not confined to dusty old books.

They were living and breathing like us. They had flaws, they struggled, they kept striving, aimed higher, and broke through into light.

But *they* weren't like *me*. They were great souls, giants. *My* faults, *my* difficulties were enormous, like the towering granite walls standing before me. How could someone like me ever break through? It was all I could do to get up in the morning, sit there fidgeting, try to focus, and keep my doubts at bay.

With these thoughts roiling my mind I felt a presence and saw movement in my peripheral vision. I turned to see Maharaji standing a few feet away, arms folded across his chest, wearing a white pajama-kurta and his cream-colored turban, long white beard blowing in the mountain breeze. I had seen him stand like that so many times over the years — overseeing volunteer work at the spiritual colony where he lived, standing among his congregation, hosting tea-parties in his garden.

His serene, smiling eyes were locked on mine, radiating love. I almost lost my footing and had to steady myself on the low rock wall.

Return

"Master?" I stammered.

"Yes."

I hadn't heard that soft, gentle voice for nearly thirty years.

"Master?" I asked again, tears welling.

"Yes?"

"It's you?"

"Yes."

He just kept looking at me with his serene, smiling, loving eyes — and I drank.

Then the mind kicked in.

"It's a very stressful and pressured life," I complained, tears welling up, "I mean, it's America, it's the twenty-first century. . . ."

"Maybe Sokrates, or Herakleitos, or the Apostles, or people like that — great souls, great seekers, living long ago — could go within, could reach There, but I mean — my question is — is it possible for someone like *me*, a normal person, knowing the type of life we lead?"

"Brother," he said sweetly, "it's not the atmosphere around, in the world — that's the same everywhere. It's only a very minor difference everywhere. It's the atmosphere in which you are living yourself, personally, within yourself. You have to build that atmosphere within yourself for meditation. You have to build that fort within yourself, in which you have to live. And that outside influence doesn't bother you, doesn't affect you. You're not concerned with outside atmosphere at all. The whole world is like that, there's no question of American."

"So it's possible to reach There before you physically die?" I asked.

"Yes," he said softly and authoritatively, "that is what our endeavor is."

Still I wasn't satisfied.

"But how, master?" I persisted, "I've been at this for a very long time now — many decades, *and nothing's happened!*"

"Nothing exceptional or dramatic happens," he answered.

"We just know the technique, how to go inward and upward, how to withdraw the mind from outside, and to concentrate at the eye center, and to be in touch with the Sound Current within."

"Nothing dramatic happens?" I asked, "How can I cut away everything — as Plotinus said — this mountain of myself — without something dramatic happening?"

"It depends upon our practice — to make it happen. Sometimes we get immediate results, or results very soon. Sometimes it takes quite a time for the mind to be drawn back to the eye center. It varies with individuals. Nothing dramatic happens."

I was overcome with gratitude for what Maharaji had given me. As a young man I was curious, seeking, but I was lost. I had read philosophy, religion — all the books I could find. But did

Return

I understand them? No. It was all a jumble. One religion covers their head to show respect, one takes their hat off. One religion shaves, one keeps long hair. Even with the best teachers and professors, it didn't make sense.

Then, the master came into my life — irresistibly attractive. Carefully he drew me in, shaping my life, guiding me — of course I didn't know it then — but now, forty years later it was plain. He explained spirituality so patiently, answering the same questions over and over for decades. He made sense of the jumble, he revealed the common spiritual core of all these religions, philosophies and teachings.

Most of all, he'd built a relationship. He loved me, and moved me to love him.

Now we were standing alone together at the edge of the overlook, the panorama of the Sierra spread out before us, and still I had doubts.

"Is it really possible, as you've been telling us, is it really possible to reach the eye center?"

"Yes, brother, why not?" he said gently, "It's not difficult at all. It's so simple and easy that a child of five or a man a hundred years old can do it without difficulty.

"Yet it is difficult in a way," he continued, "on account of our having so little hold over our mind. So to follow it is much more difficult than it looks. One has to change one's entire way of life

Yosemite Reverie

and one's attitude towards life. To follow it requires a complete transformation, so it's not easy."

"It's more than 'not easy,'" I protested, "it's impossible! I know, because I've been doing it for forty years!"

"You can say, *I am doing it* provided you are doing it," he answered with infinite patience, "but when you really do it, then you won't say, 'I am doing it.' 'I' only comes when we don't do it. When we truly meditate, then 'I' just disappears."

"You do it by not doing it?" I asked, not understanding.

"Just let go," he said, "When you close the eyes, you are there where you should be. Then, keeping your attention there, you should try to repeat the words.

"You are automatically there. When you close your eyes, you are nowhere else but there behind the eyes in the darkness. Just close your eyes. You don't have to find that spot at all. Whenever you're thinking, you're automatically there at the eye center. When you close the eyes, you are there where you should be."

I realized finally what Maharaji was saying, what they all were saying: spirituality isn't seeking, it's being. As Plotinus just told me earlier in the day, *It's a presence.* Our only task is to let go of everything else and reach for it.

"No matter who you ask," Maharaji continued, "it may be Sokrates, or Jesus, or Buddha, or anyone — our answer will

Return

always be the same, 'Come with us and see.'

"Could there be a better offer?" he added with a twinkle in his eyes.

With those words a cold wind came up, and the sky went dark. Snow began to fall. First a few flurries, light and vanishing on the ground, then heavy, thick snowflakes coming down and blowing around thick and fast. Snow dusted my eyebrows, clung to my lashes, chilled my face, covered my boots. It was falling so thick and fast I couldn't see the tourists at the other end of the overlook, or the ridges beyond. I could barely see the nearby trees and rocks and Maharaji standing a few feet from me. Everything was engulfed in a thick white swirl.

He appeared to dematerialize. First his shoes and pajama legs shimmered into white and swirled into the wind. Then the bottom of his waistcoat and kurta. He was dropping his body, cell-by-cell, bit-by-bit, into pure white snowflakes.

In a few moments his form disappeared entirely, leaving only his beard, face and turban seeming to hover above the ground. Then even they precipitated into pure white flakes, carried away by the wind. Last — his serene, smiling eyes.

He had vanished into a swirl of snow.

I looked around. No trace. It was midsummer, and out of a clear blue sky had come unnumbered snowflakes, blanketing

Yosemite Reverie

everything. Master dropped his body and merged into it.

The snow stopped and the sky opened again, clear and blue.

I turned to the panorama in front of me. Everything was covered in snow — the sheer granite walls, the tall pines and firs, the canyon with the waterfalls cascading to the valley floor. Everything was wrapped and blanketed except the black river snaking through the silent white.

The tourists at the other end of the overlook in their shorts and t-shirts didn't seem to notice. They continued snapping selfies, enjoying the view, talking and laughing. But I couldn't hear them, the thick carpet of snow deadened all sound. I was deep in thought, still doubting, questioning.

How could the day-by-day sitting, the repetition of a few words, the contemplation in the darkness, listening to the silence, the small acts of devotion and obedience — eating vegetarian, living an honest life — how could these little things carry enough power to grind away this ego, these towering doubts, these mountains of karma?

For a long time I gazed emptily at the snowy landscape, my questions reverberating across the canyons. Then I remembered John Muir's description of how the Yosemite Valley was created.

Muir, the nineteenth-century Scottish naturalist who was one of the first Europeans to scale these mountains, and whose writings inspired the movement to preserve their wildness, asked, "what force in nature could possibly have the power to take a vast, undifferentiated block of solid granite, and sculpt these majestic domes, canyons and ridges hidden within?"

"Nature chose not earthquake or lightning to rend and split asunder," he wrote, "but the tender snowflake, noiselessly falling through unnumbered centuries. Strong only by force of numbers, laboring harmoniously in united strength, they crushed and ground and wore away the rocks."

Nothing dramatic happened.

It was the pressure of glaciers — streams of closely packed snow crystals, stacked layer upon layer — that cut a single, enormous unshaped wave of solid granite into this majestic landscape. Each canyon, waterfall, dome and ridge, no matter how high or how hard, was carved out of solid rock by the gentle, persistent pressure of unmelted snow under the direction of nature's divine designer.

One snowflake was inconsequential. Yet enough of them, over a long enough period of time, had sculpted the landscape lying in front of me. It was natural. It happened slowly. It was profound, and it was easy. Maybe meditation could be like that, too. Maybe it didn't need to be a struggle. Maybe I could just sit down, let go and enjoy.

One round of repetition, one day of meditation, one act of

Yosemite Reverie

love — each seems inconsequential, too. But if agents so small and fragile as snowflakes could do this vast rock work, then what could prevent this yearning, restless soul — through gentle, persistent effort and the unerring, loving guidance of the master, the *Logos*, within — from cutting away everything, and breaking free?

I remembered another man who went to the mountains to find God, a long time ago. He also expected something dramatic:

The Lord said, go out and stand upon the mountain, for the Lord is about to pass by . . .

and behold, a great and powerful wind tore the mountains and shattered the rocks — but the Lord was not in the wind.

After the wind there was an earthquake — but the Lord was not in the earthquake.

And after the earthquake there was a fire, but the Lord was not in the fire.

And after the fire, a still small voice.

It's not a storm, not an earthquake, not a raging fire. There's no need to do anything great, or look for anything dramatic — only to show up, be present, quiet within — and pay attention.

Then, there, in the silence, it comes — *a still small voice.*

I was always busy thinking about the future, looking for

breakthroughs, trying to make a stronger effort — trying and trying harder. But meditation isn't trying. It's being.

Just close your eyes and you are where you should be.

What I was looking for doesn't lie sometime in the future, because the future never comes. The future is the realm of thought, of mind, of time. The Presence can only be experienced in the present.

As Eckhart Tolle observed,

> Why does the mind habitually deny or resist the Now? Because it cannot function and remain in control without time, which is past and future, so it perceives the timeless Now as threatening. Time and mind are in fact inseparable.
>
> Imagine the Earth devoid of human life, inhabited only by plants and animals. Would it still have a past and a future? Could we still speak of time in any meaningful way? The question, "What time is it?" or "What's the date today?" — if anybody were there to ask it — would be quite meaningless. The oak tree or the eagle would be bemused by such a question. "What time?" they would ask. "Well, of course, it's now. The time is now. What else is there?"

A sharp, high pitched shriek above broke my reverie. The dark brown V-shape swooshed past, right in front of my face, down from the towering firs behind. An iridescent yellow

Yosemite Reverie

glint of sunlight off the nape told me it was a Golden — so close I could see the intense focus in its eagle eyes.

I stood on the overlook, the canyon wall cascading almost straight down below my feet, and it soared in front of me, high above the canyon — now pumping its majestic wings flying away into the wind, now banking and sailing back in wide circles. With every shriek it called: *now . . . now . . . now.*

I took a deep breath of clear mountain air and let it out slowly. I finally got it. The questions, the doubts — they weren't resolved. They dissolved. I felt able, at last, to do what Maharaji always encouraged us to do — accept a simple thing in a simple way.

It's a seed planted inside of me — no, not inside of me, it *is* me, the real me, the eternal me, the me that stares out at these sprawling ranges and gazes within at the same time. It's the seed of life, of love, awakened by a living water, that sheds the skin of self, roots deep into the ground of being, and, pulled by the light into the light, transforms itself into a spreading tree.

All I could do — all anyone can do — is tend to the seed, cultivate the tree. Can't force it to grow — it grows by itself. Meeting a master is planting the seed. Meditation is watering the tree, merging in the Audible Life Stream is the ripening and the falling of the fruit.

Return

It's natural — breaking out of time into the timelessness of Now — transcending the gravity of space and entering the trackless spaceless One — listening, listening, listening — and slipping into the flow of the *Logos* — unfathomably deep and infinitely high.

Yosemite Reverie

Endnotes

Endnotes

Note on the Translations
All the words attributed to Herakleitos, Sokrates, Jesus and Plotinus are authentic statements translated from authoritative sources. The names 'Herakleitos' and 'Sokrates' have been rendered using the Greek spelling rather than the more common Latinized versions.* The intention is to represent these figures more closely to their historical root, and thereby give the reader an opportunity to encounter them with fresh eyes.

The dialogue between the narrator and the Apostles is imaginary, but is based on modern scholarship.

The translations do not vary substantially from more widely available renderings except where a literal translation of the underlying Greek would sound stiff or labored in modern English. For example, the passage from Plato that would literally be translated as "a smaller comes into being from a larger" is rendered here as "smaller comes from larger."

A few Greek words of particular importance are rendered differently than in more widely available translations and discussed here.

The physical characteristics of the ancients described in the narrative are inspired by historic accounts and ancient artwork.

---

* Plotinus (Πλωτῖνος), Thomas (Θωμᾶς) and Mary (Μαρία) are spelled using the same letters in both Greek and Latin. John (Ἰωάννης) and Jesus (Ἰησοῦς) are so different in Greek as to be unrecognizable.

Yosemite Reverie

Logos

The Greek noun logos (λόγος) lies at the center of both Greek philosophy and Christian doctrine. *Logos* is a common Greek word that has many mundane meanings: "account," "reckoning," "word," "measure," "teaching," "argument," or "reason," depending on context.

Herakleitos (c.500 BC), is credited with giving logos an additional, esoteric sense, the meaning of which has been debated by scholars for centuries. In Greek philosophy *Logos* is generally rendered as "Reason," which has been described by scholars as "nature steering all things from within."*

Herakleitos' Fragment 50 offers a vivid example of how the rendering of *Logos* affects meaning, reproduced here with a literal interlinear translation:

Οὐκ ἐμεῦ ἀλλὰ τοῦ λόγου ἀκούσαντας
Not to me but to logos listening

ὁμολογέειν σοφόν ἐστι, ἓν πάντα εἶναι.
to agree wise it is one everything is.

Below are translations by three scholars:
Listening not to me but to the Logos it is wise to agree that all things are One." G.S. Kirk, 1957.

"Not after listening to me, but after listening to the account, one does wisely in agreeing that all things are (in fact?) one (thing)." Robinson, T. M, 1987.

---

* Hamilton, Edith & Cairns, Huntington, eds. *Collected Dialogues of Plato*. Bollingen Series LXXI: Princeton, Seventh printing, 1973, p. xiii.

Endnotes

It is wise, listening not to me but to the report, to agree that all things are one." Kahn, Charles H., 1979.

Here *logos* is treated three different ways: untranslated, "account," and "report." The rendering used here follows the translation by G. S. Kirk of Cambridge University. It is closest to the Greek, and allows the reader to decide what *Logos* means. Professor Kirk's struggling analysis illustrates how difficult it is to assign an intellectual meaning to *logos*:

"*Logos* for Heracleitus usually means something outside himself, namely, the formula of all things . . . . On the other hand, it may be explained as referring primarily to 'of mine . . . .' Finally, it is perfectly possible that some degree of personification of *Logos* is implied: the *Logos* is present in all things, it is obvious, it 'speaks its presence' . . . ."

While *Logos* is generally rendered as "Reason" in Greek philosophy, it's rendered as "The Word" in Christian doctrine — the divine, creative power manifest in the world. The primary example of *Logos* in Christianity is found in the Prologue of the *Gospel According to John*:

Ἐν ἀρχῇ　　　ἦν　ὁ λόγος,
In the beginning　was　the logos,

καὶ ὁ λόγος　　ἦν πρὸς　τὸν θεόν,
and the logos　was with　the god

καὶ θεὸς　ἦν　ὁ λόγος.
and god　was　the logos.

Yosemite Reverie

Furthermore, while philosophical "Reason" is held in high esteem by modern commentators, the Christian "Word" is considered to be something different and superior.

For example, the *Oxford Classical Dictionary* defines *Logos* in Greek philosophy as "reason," tracing its use by philosophers from Herakleitos to Plato and beyond. However, the *Dictionary* says, in the Christian Bible *Logos* means "Word," and concludes:
> In so far as the philosophers lived according to reason they were Christians before Christ; but after Christ's coming, *Christians have the whole and undiluted truth.* [emphasis added]

From at least 500 BC through 250 AD, there was a continuous tradition of *Logos*-teachers across the Mediterranean basin, but it's impossible to see in translation, because various English words are used for the same Greek word depending on the translator's understanding, as illustrated below:

Herakleitos c. 500 BC	λόγος	"account"
Sokrates c. 400 BC	λόγος	"Reason"
John c. 100 AD	λόγος	"Word"
Plotinus c. 250 AD	λόγος	"rational principle"

It's not possible, then, to imagine an integrated stream of Greek religious and philosophical thought stretching across the centuries, because translators use different words while in the underlying texts there is only one.

However, if *Logos* is understood to be an Audible Life Stream — something that is both consciousness and the way back to source of consciousness — the meaning is clear, as is the link between these texts.

Endnotes

To make this consistency visible, and eliminate any bias favoring one *Logos* as superior to another, *Logos* is untranslated here. The intention is to make evident the possibility that all of these *Logos* teachers — whether in a philosophical or Christian context — are talking about the same thing.

I. Ascent
7   someone gave me a book, *Spiritual Gems* . . .
    During devotional practice, as the concentration improves, mind and soul vacate the body and pass through the eye centre, then cross the starry sky, *the sun, and the moon, and meet the Radiant Form of the Master. From there onwards the Master's Form acts as guide, and the journey is made in the company of the Master.* Spiritual Gems, *ltr. 23.*

8   *mantra* or *simran*
    Simran *is the "repetition of the five names given by the Master at the time of initiation, names that are associated with the five stages or regions of the inner journey;* simran *is a key aspect of the meditation process, designed to focus the mind at the eye centre.* Glossary, *Spiritual Letters* (1998 edition)

10   *upwards flows the river.* Tukaram

12   *eye focus for three hours* Spiritual Gems, ltr. 154.

16   *"Yo-sem-i-tee,"* I said outloud to myself. . . .
    Origin of the Word Yosemite by Daniel E. Anderson (December 2004;

Yosemite Reverie

last updated July 2011) http://www.yosemite.ca.us/library/origin_of_word_yosemite.html accessed 28 Feb 2018

21 *In so many lives, you were a worm and an insect* . . . Sri Guru Granth Sahib, M5 p. 176

There is a growing apprehension that existence is a rat-race in a trap . . . Watts, Alan. The Book. p. 5

II. *Glen Aulin*

Herakleitos is the first Greek philosopher known to have put *Logos* at the center of his teachings. Nothing of Herakleitos' writing survives — all we know comes from other writers quoting him in sayings known as "Fragments."

27 *You cannot step into the same river twice...* Fr. 91*, also quoted in Plato, Cratylus (402a).

The river we step in is the same, and yet it is not the same, because we both exist and we also do not exist. Fr. 49a

Everything flows... and the river is always flowing by. Fr. 12

28 *If happiness were in the pleasures of the body, we'd say that cows are happy when they find a bitter bush to eat.* Fr. 4

30 *Learning many things doesn't teach intelligence.* Fr. 40

---

* here numbered according to Diels

Endnotes

Many divine things escape being understood because of disbelief. Fr. 86

The invisible harmony is greater than anything visible. Fr. 54

Thunderbolt steers all things. Fr. 64

Although the Logos is common to all, people live as if they have their own private understanding. Fr. 2

For those who are awake, there is one Universe. But those who sleep each turn into their own private world. Fr. 89

And regarding the Logos, which is eternal, people aren't able to understand before hearing it, or even after they've heard it once. And though everything comes into being through this Logos, they're unaware of its nature, even when I show them what it is. Fr. 1

31 *People just don't get it, even when they've heard it. It's like they're deaf. We have a saying for it: 'present, yet absent.'* Fr. 34

The [barley] mix in the pot will separate if it's not stirred. Fr 125

32 *I searched myself.* Fr. 101

The road up and the road down are the same. Fr. 60

Donkeys would rather have garbage than gold. Fr. 9

33 *Life and death are the same, sleeping and waking, youth and*

Yosemite Reverie

age... these change into those and those change into these, and back again. Fr. 88

A circle begins and ends at the same point. Fr. 103

Mortals are immortals and immortals are mortals, the one living the other's death and dying the other's life. Fr. 62

34 *A man's character is his destiny.* Fr. 119

The bow is called 'life,' but the work is death. Fr. 48
A man kindles a light within himself in the night-time when his sight is extinguished. In life he touches death when sleeping, and in sleep he awakens. Fr. 26

Some people are unaware of what they do when they're awake, just as they forget what they do when they're asleep. Fr 1

Death is what we see when we're awake —all we see when we're sleeping is sleep! Fr. 21

37 *Good and bad are the same thing. To God all things are beautiful and good and just. But men have assumed some things to be just and others to be unjust.* Fr. 102

For example sea water is both pure and poisonous. For the fishes it's pure — they can drink it and it gives them life — but for men it's poisonous — it they drink it, it's fatal. Fr. 61

Endnotes

And it's not necessarily better that things turn out the way we want. Fr. 110

Disease makes us appreciate health, evil makes us appreciate good, hunger makes us appreciate abundance, and hard work makes us appreciate rest. Fr. 111

God is day-night, winter-summer, war-peace, hunger-fullness. But he changes the way fire, when mixed with spices, is like incense — named after the fragrance of each spice. Fr. 67

38 *If you don't expect the unexpected, you won't discover it — it's undiscoverable and trackless.* Fr. 18

to have success in meditation . . . Maharaj Charan Singh Ji, *Legacy of Love*, p. 331

39 *And you'll never discover the limits of the soul, even if you travel the whole Path, so deep is the* Logos. Fr. 45

Not to me, but listening to the Logos, *it's wise to agree that all things are One.* Fr. 50.

III. Ten Lakes

The encounter with Sokrates is adapted from Plato's *Phaedo* with one interpolation from *Symposium* and one from *Phaedrus*. All reference to Sokrates' words or teaching is from Plato's representation of Sokrates in his Dialogues.

The *Phaedo*, known to ancient commentators as *On the Soul*, presents a discussion between Sokrates and his disciples on the

YOSEMITE REVERIE

evening that Sokrates is to carry out the death sentence handed down by the Athenian court. Sokrates had been convicted of "introducing false gods" and "corrupting the youth." He was offered exile or exoneration if he were to recant, but instead chose to maintain his beliefs and accept execution.

The last meeting of Master and disciples, the Phaedo naturally contains Sokrates' essential, core message. It concerns the true practice of philosophy, the immortality of the soul, and its journey after death.

The conversation about the journey of the soul and the true practice of philosophy is a distillation of *Phaedo* 61-65, with the addition of one passage from Plato's *Symposium* (220c) in which Alcibiades describes Sokrates in meditation.

51 Yogananda, Paramhansa. p. 202

53 *So isn't it in deep contemplation, if anywhere at all, that it sees things as they really are?*

   And it contemplates best, I guess, whenever none of these things bothers it, not hearing or sight or pain, or any pleasure either, but whenever it comes to be alone by itself as far as possible, ignoring the body, and whenever, having the least possible association and contact with it, it strives for things as they really are.... Phaedo 65c

This is the most essential passage in the most essential of Plato's dialogues for readers interested in Sokrates' esoteric teaching.*

---
* The Greek text is presented here
ἆρ' οὖν οὐκ ἐν τῷ λογίζεσθαι εἴπερ που ἄλλοθι κατάδηλοναὐτῇ γίγνεταί τι

Endnotes

After describing the true practice of philosophy as "nothing other than practicing dying and being dead," a clear reference to meditation, Sokrates now describes how the soul can see things as they really are — direct perception of reality.

The key word is *logizesthai*, a noun, which is variously translated as *in reasoning* (Grube, Gallop), *in reflection* (Tredennick), *in mathematical reasoning* (Burnet), and *in thinking* (Fowler).

In everyday Greek *logizetai* often had the meaning "to calculate," "compute," "count," or "reckon." How can *logizetai*, then, have an esoteric meaning?

Consider the verb "to sit." In normal conversation, if someone says "to realize the truth, we must sit everyday," we might think, how can the truth be realized by sitting? and why "everyday"?

But if we know the speaker to be a teacher of a meditation, a daily practice undertaken while sitting still for long periods, then we understand that the sitting being referred to is the sitting in meditation, and the emphasis on "everyday" is an emphasis on dedicated practice. Sitting becomes a metaphorical term for meditation. Perhaps Socrates' associates would understand, when he uses a verb that means, in daily use, "to reckon" or "to think" as the way to see the things as they really are, he meant not the usual kind of reckoning or thinking, but the kind that comes from aligning the conscious attention with the Logos through meditation.

Socrates has described meditation succinctly in the immediately preceding lines as the practiced and controlled separation of

---

τῶν ὄντων;

λογίζεται δέ γέ που τότε κάλλιστα, ὅταν αὐτὴν τούτωνμηδὲν παραλυπῇ,
μήτε ἀκοὴ μήτε ὄψις μήτε ἀλγηδὼνμηδέ τις ἡδονή, ἀλλ' ὅτι μάλιστα
αὐτὴ καθ' αὑτὴνγίγνηται ἐῶσα χαίρειν τὸ σῶμα, καὶ καθ' ὅσον δύναται
μὴκοινωνοῦσα αὐτῷ μηδ' ἁπτομένη ὀρέγηται τοῦ ὄντος.

soul from body as at the time of death. How can the soul perceive "things as they really are" through the medium of the intellect, which depends on the bodily senses that Socrates has just rejected as inadequate? If the perception is through the medium of the intellect, then it's not direct perception of things "as they really are."

The presence of *log-* at the root of this key verb presents the tantalizing possibility that he is making an indirect reference to the *Logos* of Herakleitos, Jesus, Plotinus and other Greek philosophers.

In that case, *logizetai* could refer to the process of apprehending that transcendent and sublime *Logos* through deep contemplation. The rendering here — *in deep contemplation* — allows for this possibility without precluding the more intellectual, rational interpretations.

55 the *living and ensouled* Logos *of the one who knows.*
The discussion of Sokrates mistrust of words and search for a real *Logos* is an excerpt from *Phaedrus* (275d-277a).

58 The discussion of opposites and the existence of the soul after death is a distillation of *Phaedo* 70-72.

62 The discussion of reincarnation and transmigration of the soul — karma theory — is a distillation of *Phaedo* 81-84.

67 The description of the journey of the soul after death and the Spirit Guide is a distillation of *Phaedo* 107-110.

71 The description of the True Earth and the metaphysical cosmology is a distillation of *Phaedo* 111-114.

76 They see the sun and moon and stars as they really are, and they are happy in all other ways. 111c

Endnotes

81 So one should repeat these things to oneself like an incantation, which is why I've prolonged this story. 114d

85 The description of Sokrates departure is a distillation of *Phaedo* 115-118.

89 ... *Maharaji had left us, a loss too enormous to bear.*
Before his passing, Maharaj Charan Singh Ji appointed Baba Gurinder Singh Ji as his spiritual successor at the Radha Soami Satsang Beas. Baba ji, as he is known to his followers, continues the work of disseminating the spiritual teachings and inspiring his disciples towards meditation.

IV. Bhog Jooni
103 I remembered that Russian pilgrim . . .
Ceaseless interior prayer is a continuous aspiration and a yearning of the spirit of man towards God. To succeed in this sweet exercise it is necessary to ask God frequently that He teach you to pray continuously. The Way of the Pilgrim, p. 14.

Sit alone and in silence; bow your head and close your eyes; relax your breathing and with your imagination look into your heart; direct your thoughts from your head into your heart. And while inhaling say, "Lord Jesus Christ have mercy on me," either softly with your lips or in your mind. Endeavor to fight distractions but be patient and peaceful and repeat this process frequently ...."
p. 19

Yosemite Reverie

So now I walk and say the Jesus Prayer without ceasing and it is more precious and sweet to me than anything else in the world. Sometimes I walk seventy or more versts a day (~50 miles or 80 km) and I do not get tired; I am only conscious of praying. When the cold air chills me, I begin saying the Prayer with greater intensity and I warm up. When hunger begins to overcome me, I begin saying the name of Jesus Christ more frequently and I forget that I wanted to eat. When I become sick and feel rheumatic pain in my back and legs, I pay greater attention to the prayer and I do not feel the pain.... Even though I have not attained the ceaseless self-activating prayer of the heart, I now clearly understand what is the meaning of the words of the Apostle Paul, "Pray constantly."
p. 23-24

V. Smith Peak

Logos as the creative principle of Christianity comes primarily from its use in the Prologue to *The Gospel According to John*:

1 Ἐν ἀρχῇ ἦν ὁ λόγος,
καὶ ὁ λόγος ἦν πρὸς τὸν θεόν,
καὶ θεὸς ἦν ὁ λόγος.
2 οὗτος ἦν ἐν ἀρχῇ πρὸς τὸν θεόν.
3 πάντα δι' αὐτοῦ ἐγένετο,
καὶ χωρὶς αὐτοῦ ἐγένετο οὐδὲ ἕν.
4 ὃ γέγονεν 4 ἐν αὐτῷ ζωὴ ἦν,
καὶ ἡ ζωὴ ἦν τὸ φῶς τῶν ἀνθρώπων
5 καὶ τὸ φῶς ἐν τῇ σκοτίᾳ φαίνει,
καὶ ἡ σκοτία αὐτὸ οὐ κατέλαβεν.

Endnotes

1 In the beginning was the *Logos*,
and the *Logos* was with God,
and the *Logos* was God.
2 It was present with God in the beginning.
3 Through It all things came into being,
and apart from It not a thing came to be,
4 That which had come to be in It was life,
and this life was the light of men.
5 The light shines in the darkness,
and the darkness cannot comprehend it.

The scene of the Apostles singing the Prologue is inspired by the consensus among biblical scholars that it was "an originally independent poem that has been adapted to the Gospel" and sung as a hymn:

...the original poem underlying the Prologue was a hymn of the Johannine church. Hymns to Christ are mentioned in [various places] in the New Testament.... Eusebius (c. 300 AD) cites a testimony that speaks of psalms and hymns which from the beginning were sung to Christ as the Word, divinizing him.[*]

The translation of the Prologue rendered here differs from common standard English translations in two ways: retaining the word *Logos*, rather than translating it as "The Word," for the reasons noted above, and the rendering of the pronouns οὗτος and αὐτοῦ in 1:2-4, which can be either neuter and masculine, so can be rendered either as "it" or "him."

The first translation of the Greek New Testament directly into

---

[*] Brown, Raymond E. *The Gospel According to John (I-XII)*. p. 20-23.

Yosemite Reverie

English, by William Tyndale in 1526, renders these pronouns as inanimate: οὗτος as "the same" and αὐτοῦ as "it."

> 1 In the beginnynge was the worde
> and the worde was with God:
> and the worde was God.
> 2 *The same* was in the beginnynge with God.
> 3 All thinges were made by *it*
> and with out *it* was made nothinge that was made.
> 4 In *it* was lyfe and the lyfe was ye lyght of men
> 5 and the lyght shyneth in the darcknes but the darcknes comprehended it not. *[emphasis added]*

This rendition continues in the *Geneva Bible* of 1560 and the *Bishops' Bible* of 1568.

However, the version with the royal stamp of approval, the *Authorized Version*, or *King James Version* of 1611 (KJV), the most popular Bible of all time, keeps οὗτος as "the same," but renders the pronoun αὐτοῦ as animate: "him."

> 1 In the beginning was the Word, and the Word was with God, and the Word was God.
> 2 *The same* was in the beginning with God.
> 3 All things were made by *him*; and without *him* was not any thing made that was made.
> 4 In *him* was life; and the life was the light of men.
> 5 And the light shineth in darkness; and the darkness comprehended it not. *[emphasis added]*

The *New Revised Standard Version*, published in 1989, one of the most respected and widely used modern English translations, attributes both pronouns as masculine and animate: "him."

Endnotes

1 In the beginning was the Word, and the Word was with God, and the Word was God.
2 *He* was in the beginning with God.
3 All things came into being through *him*, and without *him* not one thing came into being. What has come into being
4 In *him* was life, and the life was the light of all people.
5 The light shines in the darkness, and the darkness did not overcome it. *[emphasis added]*

We see that, over time, the translation has changed to anthropomorphize the Creative Power, *Logos*. The translation of these pronouns has profound impact on meaning.

The meaning of Line 2 is a repetition of Line 1. οὗτος in the second line clearly refers to Logos. By translating οὗτος, in Line 2 as "He," and αὐτοῦ in Lines 3-4 as "him," it is understood to mean the divine Christ, of which Jesus was the incarnation. This makes little sense — Jesus didn't exist "in the beginning." He was a human being, born at a particular time, and the embodiment of *Logos* only for a particular time. *Logos* in the beginning is something else — a primal, timeless, Creative Power.

As noted in the *Oxford Encyclopedia of The Bible and Gender Studies*:

"The appearance of αὐτοῦ in v.3 refers to Logos, and since Logos is personified and inanimate, the translation of αὐτοῦ is 'it.' Thus the translators of the KJV are proposing that *Logos* (the antecedent for *autou*) is equivalent to Jesus. This is hardly a fair rendition, however. If John had seen *Logos* as Jesus, John would have used Jesus instead of *Logos*. But John didn't do this. So Tyndale, and after him the *Bishops' Bible* and the *Geneva Bible*

Yosemite Reverie

attest a rendition of *John* 1 in English that better represents the Greek."*

114 *I remember when we were confronted by the mob in the Tabernacle
. . . This is a summary of John* Chapter 8.

115 *The light shines in the darkness and the darkness can't grasp it.*
John 1:5
καὶ τὸ φῶς ἐν τῇ σκοτίᾳ φαίνει, καὶ ἡ σκοτία αὐτὸ οὐ κατέλαβεν.
The original Greek *ou katelaben* literally means "can't get arms around," or, Latinized, "cannot comprehend."

118 *His disciples said to Him: Twenty-four prophets spoke in Israel and they all spoke about You. He said to them: You have dismissed the Living One who is before you and you have spoken about the dead.*
Gospel According to Thomas 52.

If you bring forth what is within you, what you bring forth will save you. But if you do not bring forth what is within you, what you do not bring forth will destroy you. Thomas 60. [translated by MacRae, as quoted in Pagels, *Beyond Belief*, p. 32.]

119 *Jesus said, "If they say to you, 'Where did you come from?', say to them, 'We came from the light, the place where the light came into being from itself. It stood and revealed itself in their image.' If they say to you, 'Who are you?', say, "We are its children, we are the elect of the living father.' If they ask you, 'What is the sign of your father in you?', say to them, 'It is movement and repose.'"* Thomas 50.

---

* O'Brien, Julia M (ed)., *Oxford Encyclopedia of The Bible and Gender Studies*, vol 1. Oxford : Oxford University Press, 2014. ISBN 978-0-19-020488-4. p. 94-95

Endnotes

120 *But if you do not know yourselves, then you are in poverty and you are poverty.* Thomas 3.

The summary of Church history is adapted from Pagels and other sources (see Bibliography).

125 "The late Raymond Brown, a prominent New Testament scholar... stated this perspective baldly: what orthodox Christians rejected was only "the rubbish of the second century"– and, he added, "it's still rubbish." Pagels, *Beyond Belief,* p. 76-77.

127 *No man comes to the Father but by me.* John 14:6

What do you mean 'his one and only son?'

This discussion of Jesus as "the one and only son" of God is rooted in translation of *monogenes* in John 3:16:
> For God so loved the world that he gave his one and only Son, that whoever believes in him shall not perish but have eternal life. *(New International Version)*
> Οὕτως γὰρ ἠγάπησεν ὁ θεὸς τὸν κόσμον, ὥστε τὸν υἱὸν τὸν μονογενῆ ἔδωκεν, ἵνα πᾶς ὁ πιστεύων εἰς αὐτὸν μὴ ἀπόληται ἀλλ' ἔχῃ ζωὴν αἰώνιον.

Raymond Brown, respected Biblical scholar, writes in his *Introduction to the Gospel According to John,*
> "There is little Greek justification for the translation of monogenes as 'one and only' or 'only begotten.' ... *Monogenes* describes a quality of Jesus, his uniqueness. It reflects Hebrew *yahid*, 'only, precious,' ... which is used to describe Abraham's son Isaac,

Yosemite Reverie

as *monogenes* is used of Isaac in *Heb.xi.17*. Isaac is Abraham's uniquely precious son, but not his only begotten.*

Unlike older versions of the New Testament, such as the *King James Version* (1611), which translates this passage as "only begotten son," many modern English translation (such as the 1978 *New International Version*) add emphasis not in the original text — asserting his stature as the "one and only" — making the rendering less precise.

129 *everybody who says they worship Christ has a different concept.* Spiritual Perspectives I, p. 464

132 *shabd guru surat dhun chela Sri Guru Granth Sahib,* M1 p. 493

I remember that first visit to the Temple... John 2:13-16

133 *If those who lead you say to you, 'See, the kingdom is in the sky,' then the birds of the sky will precede you. If they say to you, 'It is in the sea,' then the fish will precede you. Rather, the kingdom is inside of you, and it is outside of you. When you come to know yourselves, then you will become known, and you will realize that it is you who are the sons of the living father.* Thomas, 3.

135 I mean, if we had written it all down, the amazing things he did, even the whole world could not contain all the books that we'd have written.

And there are also many other things which Jesus did, the which,

---

* Brown, Raymond E. vol 29, p. 13-14.

if they should be written every one, I suppose that even the world itself could not contain the books that should be written. John 21:25

135 *he gave me his secret teaching* . . . Gospel of Mary, 6.

VI. Return

147 *Fire, air, water and earth are in themselves soulless, and there are no other elements of the body than these four . . . .*

Since none of these have life, it would extraordinary if life came about by simply mixing them together. It is impossible, in fact, that the union of material elements should produce life . . . .

148 *Furthermore, no one would pretend that a mere chance mixing could produce such results (as the human body) — some ordering principle must be necessary, some Cause directing the mixture. That guiding principle would be Soul.*

The body — not merely because it's complex, but even if it were simple — could not exist unless there were Soul in everything, for body owes its being to the entrance of Logos into matter, and only from Soul can Logos come. Enneads, IV.7.2

When Plotinus had written anything he could never bear to go over it twice. Even to read it through once was too much for him, as his eyesight did not serve him well for reading. In writing he did not form the letters with any regard to appearance or to divide his syllables correctly, and he paid no attention to spelling.

Yosemite Reverie

Porphyry's Life of Plotinus, 8.

149 *The* Logos *is the ruler, making all. It wills things as they are, and according to* Logos *it produces even what we know as evil. It cannot desire all to be good. An artist would not make an animal all eyes, and in the same way, the* Logos *would not make all divine.*

It makes gods and also celestial spirits, the intermediate order, then men, then the animals. All is a graded succession, and this in no spirit of malice, but in the expression of a Logos *that is teeming with intellectual variety.*

We are like people ignorant of painting who complain that the colors are not beautiful everywhere in the picture. But the Artist has laid on the appropriate color to every spot. Or we are criticizing a drama because the characters are not all heroes but include a servant and a rustic and some humble clown. Yet take away the low characters and the power of the drama is gone. These are part and parcel of it. Enneads, III.2.11

150 *If this universe is the direct creation of the* Logos *applying itself, completely unchanged, to Matter . . . then its product must be excellent and perfect . . . .*

. . . . Hence arises that awesome word, Adrasteia [Ἀδράστεια] — *the Inescapable. For in truth this arrangement is Inescapable: absolute justice and an awesome wisdom* Enneads, III.2.12-13

152 *It's like this: the visible Sokrates is a man . . . . and this outer*

Endnotes

Logos *has a similar relationship to the truest* Logos *of man. And so much for that.* Enneads, VI.3.15

153 Logos *is the beginning and* Logos *is everything and everything is generated by it and arranged at birth entirely in this way.* Enneads, III.2.15

Life and thought and all things come from the One, and It — the One — is not one of those things, but all things come from It — because It is formless. That One is One alone." Enneads, V.1.7

154 *What then is our way of escape, and how are we to find it? . . . Our country from which we came is There, our Father is There. How shall we travel to it? Where's our way of escape?*
We cannot get There on foot — our feet only carry us around in this world, from one land to another. You mustn't ride a carriage, either, or a boat. Let all these things go — don't even look at them. Shut your eyes — change to — wake up to another way of seeing — a way of seeing that everybody has available to them but few actually develop.

And what does this inner sight see? At first — when it's just awakened — it's not at all able to look at the brilliance before it. So the soul must be trained — first of all to see the beautiful way to live, then and the beautiful way to act — not like the things people make, but the work of men who are called truly Good, then finally at the souls of those who are truly beautiful.

How, then, can you see the sort of beauty a good soul has?

154 well-known lines from the Sikh gurus, *Sri Guru Granth Sahib*, M2 p. 139

Yosemite Reverie

155 *Withdraw into yourself and look — and if you don't see beauty within your-self, then, just like someone who makes a beautiful statue cuts here and polishes there, and makes one part smooth and clears another until he's made a beautiful face, so you also have to cut away excess and straighten the crooked and clear the dark and make it bright, and never stop working on your statue until the divine glory of virtue shines out of you, till you've achieved self-mastery!*

If you've become this, and see it, and are at home with yourself in purity — with nothing stopping you from becoming One like this, with no inward mixture of anything else, but entirely yourself, nothing but True Light — immeasurable, boundless, limitless — everywhere unmeasured — because greater than all measure and better than all quantity — when you see that you have become this — then you have become sight itself — you can trust yourself then, you have already ascended and need no one to show you — concentrate your gaze and see! Enneads, I.6.8-9

156 . . . he had broken into a light sweat. I found myself deeply attracted to his face.
When he was speaking his intellect visibly lit up his face. There was always a charm about his appearance, but at these times he was even more attractive to look at. He sweated gently, and a kindliness shone out from him, and in answering questions he made clear both his benevolence to the questioner and his intellectual vigor. Porphyry, Life of Plotinus, 13.

157 *There's nothing random or by chance . . . . And that same thing is lovable and love — and love of himself — for he is beauty of himself*

Endnotes

and in himself— nothing else! Enneads VI.8.14-15

Everything that exists has its existence by the One.

The biggest puzzle is that understanding of the One is neither by reasoning nor by intellectual perception. It's rather a presence superior to knowledge.

In what sense do we call it "One"? . . .

The One isn't ... indivisible, as if it were the smallest thing. It's the greatest of all things – not in extension, but in power.

158 *And it must be understood as infinite not because its size and number can't be measured or counted but be-cause its power can't be comprehended.*

When you think of it as God or as mind— it's more — it's more than you imagine it to be – for it exists in itself – without attributes....

And it has no place, for it has no need of a place. Other things come to a place because of the One. Because of it, they exist at the same time as they take up their assigned place. To seek a place is to be in need, and the Source is not in need of the things that come after it . . . The source of all things has no need for anything. . . .

It's not mind . . . nor motion . . . since it's prior to motion and mind. Indeed, what should it understand? Itself? It alone neither knows nor does it have anything which it doesn't know — but being One and One with itself, it doesn't need thought of itself.

Yosemite Reverie

Don't form your vision by diverting your thought elsewhere. It doesn't lie somewhere . . . but is always present to anyone who's able to touch it. Enneads VI.9.1-7

159 *We may know we have had the vision when the Soul has suddenly taken light. This light is from the Supreme and it is the Supreme. . . . And how is this to be accomplished? Cut away everything.* Enneads V.3.17

165 *If you ask the name of the Lord, it is love, love, and love.* Spiritual Discourses II, p. 146-7

You cannot hustle the Power within. Science of the Soul, ltr. 94

173 I mean, it's America, it's the twenty-first century. . . .
Q. [emotional] Master... many years ago you told me that if you wanted to have your own personal Lord inside, you have to contact the Radiant Form.

Now, I'm American, and, as you know, Americans can live a very stressful and pressured life...

I can understand how Mira Bai could come to the Radiant Form, but my question is, can someone like me, or an American, attain the Radiant Form...? Is it possible for us to go within knowing the type of life we lead, or is it something you can only look forward to when you die, your physical death?

A. Sister, it is not the atmosphere around, in the world — that is the same everywhere. It is only a very minor difference everywhere. It is the atmosphere in which you are living yourself,

Endnotes

personally, within yourself. Whether how much you are influenced by that atmosphere within yourself. You have to build that atmosphere within yourself for meditation. You have to build that fort within yourself, in which you have to live. And that outside influence doesn't bother you, doesn't affect you. You're not concerned with outside atmosphere at all.

Q. So then it could be done?

A. You have to be strong enough within yourself, not to be affected by any atmosphere. Or, if you have to go around, they are affected with your influence rather than you are infected by their influence. Everybody has to build his own fort in which one has to live. If you are always expecting the atmosphere will become better, then perhaps we will never meditate. The whole world is like that, there's no question of American.

Q. So it's possible to reach the radiant form before you physically die?

A. Yes, that is what our endeavor is.

Q. Thank you. Maharaj Charan Singh Ji, Bombay 1988 (transcribed from audio recording)

174 nothing dramatic happens . . .
Q. What needs to happen to a disciple between the time they're first initiated ... and the time they're ready to go in?

A. Well, brother, nothing exceptional or dramatic happens. We just know the technique, how to go inward and upward, how to withdraw the mind from outside, and to concentrate

Yosemite Reverie

> *at the eye center, and to be in touch with the Shabd and Nam within. Now it depends upon our practice-- to make it happen. Sometimes, due to our past sanskaras, we get immediate results, or results very soon. Sometimes it takes quite a time for the mind to be drawn back to the eye center. It varies with individuals. Nothing dramatic happens.* Huzur Maharaj Charan Singh Ji, Bombay 1988 (transcribed from audio recording)

175 so easy that a child of five or a man a hundred . . . *Die to Live*, p. 133.

Yet it is difficult in a way . . . *Spiritual Gems,* ltr. 32

176 You can say I'm doing it. . . *Die to Live*, p. 348

When you close the eyes, you are there where you should be. *Die to Live*, p. 136

177 'Come with us and see.' *Spiritual Gems*, ltr. 116.

Could there be a better offer? *Spiritual Gems,* ltr. 105

179 Nature chose not earthquake or lightning to rend and split asunder. . .

> *It is hard to realize the magnitude of the work done on these mountains by glaciers, which are only streams of closely compacted snow crystals....The pre-glacial condition of the range was simple: one vast wave of stone in which a thousand mountains,*

Endnotes

domes, canyons, ridges...lay concealed. And in the development of these Nature chose for a tool, not the earthquake or lightning to rend and split asunder, but the tender snow...noiselessly falling through unnumbered centuries...Laboring harmoniously in united strength, they crushed and ground and wore away the rocks....This vast job of rock-work was done by agents so fragile and small as [snow-flakes]...Strong only by force of numbers, they carried away entire mountains, particle by particle, block by block, and...sculptured, fashioned, [and] modeled all the range. John Muir, abridged from *Yosemite and the Sierra Nevada*, p. 6-7.

180 Still small voice. 1 Kings 19

181 Why does the mind habitually deny or resist the Now? *The Power of NOW*, p. 34.

182 Ripening of the fruit... *Spiritual Letters*, ltr. 45.

Bibliography

Bacovin, Helen (tr.) *The Way of a Pilgrim and The Pilgrim Continues His Way.* Garden City, NY: Image Books, 1978.

Brown, Raymond E. (ed. Moloney, Francis J.) *An Introduction to the Gospel According to John.* Yale Anchor Bible, New Haven and London: Yale University Press, 2003.

____ *The Gospel According to John, I—XII, Introduction, Translation and Notes.* Yale Anchor Bible, vol 29, New Haven and London: Yale University Press, 2008.

____ *The Gospel According to John, XII-XXI, Introduction, Translation and Notes.* Yale Anchor Bible, vol 29A, New Haven and London: Yale University Press, 2008.

Davidson, John. *The Gospel of Jesus: In Search of His Original Teachings* (revised). New Delhi: Science of the Soul Research Centre, 2004.

Douglas, J. D. (ed). *The New Greek-English Interlinear New Testament.* Wheaton, Illinois: Tyndale House Publishers, Inc., 1990.

Guillaumont, A. et. al. (tr), *The Gospel According to Thomas.* New York: Harper & Row, 1959.

Hammond, N.G.L & Scullard, H.H. (eds). *The Oxford Classical Dictionary* (2nd ed). Oxford: Oxford University Press, 1970.

Handwerk, Brian. "Oldest Apostle Images Revealed by Laser," in *National Geographic.* published June 26, 2010. https://news.nationalgeographic.com/news/2010/06/photogalleries/100624-oldest-apostle-christian-icon-religion-pictures/

Heraclitus (Robinson, T. M. tr). *Fragments: a Text and Translation with Commentary.* Toronto: University of Toronto Press, 1987.

____ (tr unknown). *The Fragments of Heraclitus.* Bray: The Guild Press, 1976.

Bibliography

John, Chris (ed). *Jesus and the Apostles: Christianity's Early Rise.* New York: National Geographic Society, 2014 (ISBN 1536-6596).

Kahn, Charles H., *The art and thought of Heracleitus: an edition of the fragments with translation and commentary.* Cambridge: Cambridge University Press

King, Karen L. *The Gospel of Mary of Magdala: Jesus and the First Woman Apostle.* Santa Rosa, Calif: Polebridge Press, 2003.

Kirk, G. S., Raven, J. E., & Schofield, M. *The Presocratic Philosophers* (2nd ed). Cambridge: Cambridge University Press, 1983.

Liddell, H. G. & Scott, *Greek-English Lexicon.* Oxford: Clarendon Press, 1889 (1975 impression).

Mauk, Charlotte E (ed). *Yosemite and the Sierra Nevada, photographs by Ansel Adams, Selections from the Works of John Muir.* Houghton Mifflin Company: Boston, 1948.

Meyer, Marvin (ed). *The Nag Hammadi Scriptures: The Revised And Updated Translation Of Sacred Gnostic Texts.* New York: Harper Collins, 2007.

O'Brien, Julia M (ed)., *Oxford Encyclopedia of The Bible and Gender Studies*, vol 1. Oxford : Oxford University Press, 2014.

Pagels, Elaine. *Beyond Belief: the Secret Gospel of Thomas.* New York: Random House, 2003.

____ *The Gnostic Gospels.* New York: Vintage Books, 1981.

____ *The Johannine Gospel in Gnostic Exegesis.* Atlanta: Scholars Press, 1989.

Plato (Burnet, J. ed). *Euthyphro, Apology of Socrates, Crito.* Oxford: Oxford University Press, 1977.

____ (Grube, G.M.A. tr). *Republic.* Indianapolis: Hackett Publishing Company, 1974.

_____ (Hamilton, E. & Cairns, H. eds). *The Collected Dialogues.* Princeton: Princeton University Press, 1973.

_____ (Gallop, D. tr). *Phaedo.* Oxford: Clarendon Press, 1975.

_____ (Grube, G.M.A. tr). *Phaedo.* Indianapolis: Hackett Publishing Company, 1977.

_____ (Hackforth, R. tr). *Phaedo.* Cambridge, UK: Cambridge University Press, 1955 (1998 ed).

_____ (Burnet, J. ed). *Phaedo.* Oxford: Oxford University Press, 1911 (1963 ed). accessed at https://archive.org/stream/platosphaedo00platuoft#page/n9/mode/1up

_____ (Fowler, H. N. tr), *Euthyphro, Apology, Crito, Phaedo, Phaedrus.* Loeb Classical Library, Cambridge: Harvard University Press, 1990.

_____ (Cooper, John M., ed.). *Complete Works.* Indianapolis: Hackett Publishing Company, 1997.

_____ (Burnett, J. tr). *Opera.* Oxford: Oxford University Press, 1979.

Plotinus (tr. A. H. Armstrong). *Enneads, including Porphyry's Life of Plotinus.* Loeb Classical Library, Cambridge, MA: Harvard University Press, 1966.

_____ (ed Gerson, Lloyd P). *The Enneads.* Cambridge: Cambridge University Press, 2018.

Singh, Maharaj Charan. *Die to Live.* Punjab: Radha Soami Satsang Beas, 1979.

_____ *Light on Saint John.* Punjab: Radha Soami Satsang Beas, 1985.

Singh, Maharaj Jagat, *The Science of the Soul.* Radha Soami Satsang Beas, 1982.

Singh, Baba Jaimal. *Spiritual Letters.* Punjab: Radha Soami Satsang Beas, 1998.

Bibliography

Singh, Maharaj Sawan. *Spiritual Gems: extracts from letters to seekers and disciples*. Punjab: Radha Soami Satsang Beas, 1965 (1974 ed).

Suzuki, Daisetz Teitaro. *An Introduction to Zen Buddhism*, New York: Grove Press, 1964.

Tolle, Eckhart. *The Power of Now*. Novato:New World Library, 2004.

Trine, Ralph Waldo. *In Tune With the Infinite or Fullness of Peace, Power and Plenty*. Boston: Thomas Y. Crowell & Company, 1897.

Tuckett, Christopher. *The Gospel of Mary*. Oxford: Oxford University Press, 2007.

Watts, Alan. *The Book on the Taboo Against Knowing Who You Are*. New York: Vintage Books, 1972 ed.

_____ *Do you do it or does IT do you? how to let the universe meditate you* [Audio recordings], Boulder, Colorado: Sounds True, 2005.

Yogananda, Paramhansa. *The Divine Romance, collected talks an essays on realizing God in daily life*. v. II. Los Angeles: Self-Realization Fellowship, 2017.

www.ingramcontent.com/pod-product-compliance
Lightning Source LLC
Chambersburg PA
CBHW031639040426
42453CB00006B/148